FOR SALE BY OWNER

FOR SALE BY OWNER
Sell your own home and save thousands

Russell Oddy

International Self-Counsel Press Ltd.
Head and Editorial Office
Vancouver
Toronto   Seattle

Printed in Canada

First edition: June, 1980

Canadian Cataloguing in Publication Data

Oddy, Russell, 1916-
    For sale by owner

    (Self-counsel series)
    ISBN 0-88908-065-8

    1. House selling - Canada.   I. Title.
II. Series.
HD1379.032   333.33'0971   C80-091168-7

International Self-Counsel Press Ltd.
Head and Editorial Office
306 West 25th Street
North Vancouver, British Columbia V7N 2G1
Telephone: (604) 986-3366
Vancouver   Toronto   Seattle

TABLE OF CONTENTS

LIST OF SAMPLES

INTRODUCTION

Even in these "do-it-yourself days" there are many tasks that we are unable to undertake ourselves — removing our own appendix, performing heart surgery, or pulling teeth, to name a few, although I did read of one lone "round the world" yachtsman who extracted his own molars. However, if you are anyone other than a lone boater, you would be further ahead by seeking professional assistance.

There are, however, many jobs that we can do for ourselves, things that cost a great deal of money when performed for us by others. In many cases these are deliberately shrouded in mystery in an obvious attempt to discourage the amateur.

ONE OF THESE IS THE DISPOSAL OF YOUR REAL ESTATE.

Many articles and pamphlets have been published on the subject, but something as complex as selling real estate needs much more than a leaflet. There is a lot more to it than cutting lawns and making sure that the toilets are flushed.

The purpose of this book is not to make a real estate expert out of you, but to explain in simple lay terms what and what not to do, and to help you succeed where so many others have failed. How many "For Sale by Owner" signs have you seen erected in your neighborhood, only to be replaced a few weeks later by a realtor's board, when the owner has given up in despair, many advertising dollars in the hole, resigned to paying a large real estate commission?

I am quite convinced that any person of average intelligence, who carefully follows the steps as set out in this book, can bring the sale of their property to a successful conclusion, and save thousands of dollars (and remember, tax free dollars to boot).

1
PREPARATION FOR SALE

The whole of this book could very well be termed preparation for sale, because each step that you go through is a step in that direction, whether it be cutting the front lawn, learning about the various kinds of agreements for sale and offers of purchase, or reading something about mortgage financing. However, for the time being just consider the physical aspects of the preparation process.

I have set the various steps out, not in order of importance, but in order of priority. I reiterate, this is a step-by-step operation, so let's not jump from one thing to another. For instance, it's of little use starting an advertising campaign if the front of the house needs painting, so forget the chapter on advertising until you have studied the earlier ones. Dismiss any preconceived ideas you may have with regard to selling your house. Wasn't it William Shakespeare who in *Henry V* said, "All things are ready if your mind be so?"

a. MAKE READY

For some reason or other, you have decided to sell your home; maybe your family has outgrown it and you need more living space, perhaps a change in employment is moving you out of town, or then again, maybe you are retiring and do not require all the space that you have. Whatever the reason, and it is as well to have a specific one, make sure that you let people know, otherwise they may suspect that it is the smell from the refinery or the basement that floods in the spring. And, whatever the reason, do not rush out and put a "For Sale" sign on your front lawn or pour money into the coffers of your local journal without taking the appropriate first steps. The "make ready" stage is probably the most important of them all,

1

ignorance of which is one of the reasons why most private sales fail and wind up in the realtor's hands.

First, take a good hard look at the property. Try to view it through the eyes of a stranger. Walk up the front path. Is the paving level? Could the driveway stand a couple of dollars worth of black top? Is the grass trimmed neatly? Are the flower beds free of weeds? What about the fences, do they need painting or fixing?

What about the house itself — eavestroughs O.K.? Nothing looks worse than peeling eavestroughs. Are there any other signs of neglect? Are roof tiles missing, other paintwork peeling, screens torn or damaged in any way? At this point it is a good idea to have a clip board handy and to make careful notes of any defects of this nature. Treat the rear yard in the same fashion. Does the patio need levelling? Are there any cracked paving stones that need replacing? Do trees or hedges require trimming?

Remember always, the first impressions are the most important. No car company worth its salt would show you their product as it will spend most of its life: spattered with mud, dusty, and with rust spots showing through. Their automobiles are polished and gleaming, so take a leaf from their book, let your property gleam; time and patience are all that's required.

Now let us walk into the house. Is the front door O.K.? No finger marks? If it is storm door season, make sure that you can see through it. Check the front hall. Is the hall closet neatly stowed? A cluttered closet looks a lot smaller than a neat one. Take a good look at the decor. You may love that black or purple ceiling, but 999 people out of every 1 000 will not, so paint it white.

If any redecoration is required, keep the colors as neutral as possible; this will make the interior more acceptable to the viewer. I can recall showing a house with a master bedroom in bright mauve and one wall covered in plump medieval nudes. Needless to say, I did not make the sale. Remember that all of us, or most of us, see things only as they are and not as what we could make of them.

As far as the general interior of the house is concerned, ensure that it is as sparkling as possible, particularly bathrooms and kitchens. Check out all cupboards, crawl spaces and storage areas, fix any dripping taps. That stain on the ceiling may have been caused by Jimmy shaking a pop bottle before opening it, but to a prospective buyer, it looks awfully like a leaky roof, so paint it. And avoid "the lived-in look." To outsiders, it looks like downright untidiness. No car company would try to sell an automobile full of cracker crumbs, gum wrappers or overflowing ashtrays. They would not tolerate this mess and would clear it up before the customers arrive. You must do the same.

These small, common-sense chores will cost little, but will certainly mean a lot in terms of the sale value of the house.

By the way, that *Penthouse* centre-fold over the work bench may afford the boys a treat, but may shock some people's sensibilities. Remember, you do not know the folks you are about to entertain, so play it safe and assume that they are shockable — put questionable items away in a drawer somewhere.

So, at long last you consider your property all "ship shape," just about as sparkling as you can possibly make it. The next step is to ask some very good friends or relatives to take a look and give you their honest opinion. Get them to inspect every nook and cranny as if they were about to purchase the property, and ask them to tell you what is wrong with it. There is bound to be something. Remember you have lived with certain petty annoyances for many years and have become accustomed to them: that sliding door that sticks, the cupboard door that creaks in agony, and numerous other things of this nature that you have ignored. It takes a non-resident to point them out. Before proceeding, ensure that these things are corrected; after all, you have been promising yourself that you would fix a few items around the house, and now is the time to do it.

b. FACTS AND FIGURES

The next stage in the "make ready" is to gather up your facts and figures. Check the size of your lot (this is usually on your tax bill; if not, your city hall will gladly give you this information). It is a cardinal sin to state that your frontage is 65 feet (19 1/2m), when in fact it is only 60 (18m). Many a sale has gone down the drain because of mistakes of this nature. Unfortunately, this type of error is not discovered until the purchaser's lawyer has searched the title to the property, and as this could be several weeks after the contract has been signed, much time would have been wasted during which you had considered the property sold, when in actual fact it was not.

Make sure that you have a list of all room sizes; people like to know these dimensions to ascertain whether or not their furniture will fit. Likewise, the window sizes should be on your list. Check the distances to schools, stores, and bus stops. It is pointless and deceiving to declare that the schools or whatever are only five minutes away, when that distance can be travelled in that time only at a fast sprint.

Other questions you may be asked are: How old is the house? How old is the roof? Are you on city water, main sewers or septic system? Are the pipes of the plumbing of copper? What is the amperage of your electrical system? Write the answers to all these questions down on a scratch pad, to enable anyone in the family who happens to be showing the house to answer with some authority. You may think these details are irrelevant, but in actual fact they are very necesary. You will be surprised how little you know about the house you live in once you start delving into these questions. Be meticulous; remember you are about to save, or try to save, several thousands of tax free dollars. Bear in mind that a dollar saved is a dollar earned; you are working for yourself, so do as good a job as possible.

There are many other posers your prospective purchaser will have for you, such as the annual taxes, the amount of the mortgage, (is it transferable?), the monthly payments, the interest rate. Your mortgage company and your taxation office will gladly supply these answers. If you are able to discuss the property with authority and in an intelligent fashion, this will inspire confidence in your prospective purchaser. Have all these facts and figures at hand.

In section e. I have compiled a list of the type of questions you are liable to be asked. Of course, I cannot supply the answers, only you can do that, so research carefully, and if you can think of any other points that may be brought up, add those to your list.

c. KNOW THYSELF

"It's a kind of a one-floor house with two bedrooms in the attic," or "It's on one floor but the basement is sort of at ground level." You are answering the phone, and in the first reply you are more than likely describing what is known as a "storey-and-a-half house." In the second, your stumbling description is that of an "elevated ranch."

You need to be able to identify the type of house you live in with some degree of accuracy, so read this section, decide on the style of house that you are selling and stick with that description. To the best of my knowledge, there are about 20 different types of homes of the standard kind, any one of which could describe yours. Anything else would have to be a castle or a mansion, or something of that sort. At this point, we are not taking type of construction into account, as a bungalow is a bungalow whether it is built of frame, brick or concrete block. Construction materials are discussed in the next section.

1. The bungalow

This is a one-floor building with basement. Generally, the front entrance is on one side of the house, this arrangement being the most practical one, as this provides for a larger living room. It usually has three bedrooms, bathroom, kitchen with eating area, and in many cases the living room is long enough to permit a "dining" end. Bungalows are normally sited end on to the road. If there is a garage, it is usually of the unattached type, located a little back and behind the house. Never refer to a bungalow as a ranch home, or vice versa.

2. The ranch home

Again we have one floor, but this time with the longest aspect facing the road. It is longer than the traditional bungalow. Some have the front door in the centre of the house, and this would indicate a separate dining room. In most cases, however, the main entrance is to one side, with the living room having an el-shaped dining area. The basements are quite enormous, as they run the full length of the house. Generally speaking, the average number of bedrooms on the ground level is three, with all the usual facilities on this same floor. Sometimes you will have an extra or fourth bedroom in the basement. Most ranchers have an attached garage, either double or single. This adds to the long, low appearance.

3. The elevated ranch

This is very similar to the standard ranch home, in that the living space is all on one floor. However, the difference is that the basement is at ground level, and the overall appearance is that of a two-storey home.

4. The storey-and-a-half

This could very well be described as a bungalow with living space under the roof. In other words, the attic has been utilized and dormer windows installed in the roof. The ceilings in these upper rooms slope, following the contour of the roof. In some of the older downtown areas, one will see "two-and-a-half storey" homes. However, the erection of these has been discontinued during the last quarter of a century.

5. The two storey
Never confuse a two-storey home with a storey-and-a-half. The two storey refers to two complete floors, with no sloping ceilings.

6. Three-level side split
The living room and kitchen, and so on, are on the ground floor, the family room is four or five steps down, and the bedrooms four or five steps up. Usually, the space under the living room, which is at the same level as the floor of the family room is termed "the crawl space," as it is usually only a metre or so high.

7. Four-level side split
Similar to the three-level split, except that the crawl space referred to above has been excavated to provide extra living room.

8. The back split
The back split, like the bungalow, presents its narrowest aspect to the road. As a rule, the living room and front entrance are in this section, with the bulk of the house being at the rear. It has exactly the same short stairways up and down as the side split, except that they are at the back of the house instead of the side. It can be three or four levels.

9. Semi-attached
The end units on row or town houses are referred to as semi-attached.

10. Semi-detached
Two homes with a common wall in the middle.

11. Town houses
When more than two houses are attached, side by side with common walls, they are referred to as town houses or sometimes as row houses.

12. Link homes
These houses are, to all intents and purposes, single unattached buildings, and can be in the various styles described. However, they are linked underground at the foundations. This form of construction is adopted to enable the builder to squeeze two homes on a lot where local by-laws would only permit the building of one normal dwelling.

13. The duplex
A two-family structure under one roof is referred to as a duplex. The units can be side by side, like the semi-detached house, or the second unit can be above the first, rather like a two-storey home. Both units have to be complete; the sharing of facilities such as kitchens or bathrooms "does not a duplex make." An extension of this form of accommodation is the triplex, which, as its name implies, has three units. Then, of course, we have the fourplex and fiveplex. Anything above a fiveplex, in other words six or more units, is referred to as an apartment building. A word of caution while on the subject of multi-family dwellings. If you happen to be involved in the disposal of this type of property, make sure that you have the right zoning. Check with your city hall, because if it proves to be non-conforming use you cannot sell it as other than a single family dwelling.

14. Colonial
Colonial is a loose term that originally referred to the type of house favored by plantation owners in the Deep South. They are known in the trade as "cotton-pickers' cottages." Any home that simulates this type of building is dubbed a colonial. Overly high, with pillars at the front reaching from the ground to the soffits, they boast stone steps to a

central entrance, and sometimes lattice windows. If your home is a reduced version of Tara in *Gone With the Wind*, then you have a colonial.

15. Century home

Many houses that are referred to as "century homes" have been built since 1900, so if your house falls into this category, do not call it a "century home," but rather a "mature property." No erection should be classed as a "century home" unless it is at least 100 years old.

16. Country property

Never refer to your property as "country" just because there is a field out back. It is only a country property if there are fields and farms as far as the eye can see.

17. Cape Cod

This home derives its name from the style of building once popular with residents of the east coast, and is basically a glorified version of the storey-and-a-half. It has two or more peaked dormer windows in the roof, and its longest aspect faces the road. The plan is of the centre hall type, with the dining room on the one side and the living room on the other.

18. The mansard

This could be almost any type of one-floor or split-level house, with a mansard roof. Try to imagine a house with a hat on that is pulled down over its ears, and you have the mansard. One advantage of this type of roof is the fact that one can paint the eavestroughs without the use of a step ladder.

19. The condominium

If the home that you are selling is a condominium type, you are faced with something a little different from the disposal of normal freehold property, so much so, that I feel a chapter on this subject is required (see chapter 7). The term condominium refers to a type of ownership rather than a style of house.

Bear in mind that in describing the foregoing properties, I have generalized quite a bit. For instance, if your ranch home happens to be end on to the road, it is still a ranch home. By the same token, if your bungalow reveals its longest aspect, it is still a bungalow.

If your style of property does not seem to appear in the foregoing, then you will have to decide for yourself what to term it. If in any doubt, downplay it; better to call it a cottage than a ranch home.

d. WHAT IS IT MADE OF?

Several types of construction materials are used in home building. Of necessity, the original settlers' abodes were made of logs, and due to the fact that wood was readily available, wooden or frame homes were the most common for many years. There are very few frame homes erected these days, although there are many in use.

If your home happens to be of frame construction, it could have aluminum siding. Point out this fact, as aluminum siding does not require painting or maintenance, and this is a good selling point. Another form of siding over frame, which, however, has fallen into disfavor, is insul brick. This is little more than a heavy tar paper or felt that is shaped and coloured to simulate bricks. If you have this form of siding and your prospect objects, make a selling point of it for it has one real advantage: it is an excellent insulant.

Concrete blocks were used quite extensively at one time, and these were usually covered in stucco, a form of rough cast plastering. If you are not certain what you have under that stucco, look around the house — you will find a crack somewhere that will reveal what is underneath. For goodness sake, don't claim that yours is stucco over block if you discover wood or lathe underneath.

At the turn of the century, most homes were either of frame or solid brick construction. This latter, however, is seldom used today; apart from the economic reason, solid brick is somewhat difficult to insulate. You can assume that any brick house that is 40 or more years old is solid, whereas modern houses that have the appearance of solid brick, are in fact of brick veneer. The method adopted in this form of construction is as follows: the framing is erected, the roof installed, then the exterior of the framing is covered with some kind of pressed board. The external brickwork is then laid from the foundation up with securing pieces at intervals to keep it in place. There is nothing wrong with this type of construction; in fact, it has several advantages. it is less costly, quicker to erect, and has good insulating properties. There is an outer brick wall behind which there is tar paper or some other form of damp repellent, then there is the pressed board. In between each frame on the inside there is styrofoam sheeting, then, of course, the plaster on the inner walls. Take a look at homes under construction and you will see what I mean.

Whatever the type of construction or siding that you are trying to sell, there will always be some who object, particularly if it happens to be frame. If I had a client who liked the house I had just shown, but demurred over the construction, my rejoinder would be, "This house will be standing long after we and our children are gone." Most would see the sense in this remark and drop their objection. So don't be put off by this kind of protest.

While on the topic of construction, a word or two on foundations would be in order. There are two basic types of foundation in general use; the more common is concrete block and the other poured concrete. It is as well to know what yours is, as you are bound to be asked. Another type of foundation that once was in use was that of crushed stone in a concrete-type mix. They can be seen in many of the older homes; they were usually very damp, as they were extremely porous. Once upon a time basements were just repositories for a monstrous coal-burning furnace and for the storage of coal. Nowadays, they are much more sophisticated and form part of the living space.

e. WHO, WHAT, WHY, WHEN?

Who built the house? What are the taxes? Why are you selling? When will you be moving? Questions, questions: you will be asked a million of them and you will be expected to know the answers. I have already stressed the importance of this, and to assist you in getting your facts and figures together I will list as many of the questions that you are likely to be asked as I can think of. WRITE THE ANSWERS DOWN. You may have to do some research, so get cracking now. Whatever you do, make sure that you have the right answers, not "I think so" or "perhaps," or "maybe." If any other points occur to you that are not listed, add them.

You will find most of the answers around the house somewhere. It may mean a little crawling and foraging. Anything the house cannot answer, your city hall or your mortgage company will know. It might be a good idea to remove these pages and attach them to a clip board. Fill in the answers before you start any advertising campaign.

f. PRICING

Each step in the preparation for sale is as important as the next. Private sellers go wrong somewhere along the line; the exclusion of any of the stages in this process is one of the reasons they fail, though which one they miss we will never know — they will not tell us. You are not going to fail, however, because you are going to treat each step as meticulously as the last.

It is only human to want to obtain as much as possible for your property, but not always practical if you really want to sell. We all have inflated ideas of value when it applies to something belonging to us. Your home has a certain market value, as do all homes, so perhaps it would be as well to discuss market value before we go any further.

HOUSE INFORMATION

Age of house _____

Age of roof _____

Air Conditioner: Type _____

Make _____

Age _____

Amperage _____

Annual taxes _____

Area (residential or other) _____

Aspect (Which way does the house face) _____

Assessment _____

Basement, height of _____

Broadloom _____

Builder's name _____

Construction: Brick _____ Brick Veneer _____ Frame _____ Other _____

Depth of lot _____

Distance to: Schools _____

Shopping _____

Bus routes _____

Churches _____

Recreational facilities _____

Downtown _____

Electricity, cost of _____

Exterior finish _____

Foundation, type of _____

Frontage of lot _____

Furnace: Make _____ Age _____

Fuse box location _____

Garbage collection _____

Garden, size of _____

Gas, cost of _____

Glazing, single or double _____

Heating: Gas _____ Oil _____ Other _____

Heating, cost of _____

How long have you lived in the house? _____

Insulation, type of _____

Interior finish: Plaster _____ Dry Wall _____ Other _____

Kitchen, style of _____

Mortgage: Amount _____
     Interest rate _____
     Monthly payments _____
     When due _____

Mil rate _____

Plumbing: Copper _____ Lead _____

Possession Date _____

Prevailing wind _____

Sewers or septic _____

Sidewalks _____

Size of rooms _____

_____

_____

_____

Size of windows _____

_____

_____

_____

Square footage of house _____

Square footage of lot _____

Soil, type of _____

Type of house: Bungalow _____ Side Split _____ Ranch _____ Other _____

Vacant land nearby: What is zoning _____
        What is to be built? _____

Vegetation, type of: _____

Water: Mains _____ Well _____ Other _____

Why are you selling? _____

Zoning: Present _____
   Possibility of changes _____

Market value is the price that a willing knowledgeable purchaser will pay an equally knowledgeable vendor for whatever he or she is selling. Let's say $60 000 is the proven value of a certain piece of property. If our two knowledgeables agree to this figure, then bingo, we have a true market value. However, if some unknowledgeable nitwit comes along and plunks down $100 000 for the same hunk of real estate, this would not represent a true market value. By the same token, if our $60 000 home was disposed of by an equally unknowledgeable vendor for $25 000, again, we do not have a true figure as to the worth of the property. How do you arrive at this magical, mystical figure?

There are several methods used by professional appraisers; two of the most common are the "comparative method" and the "replacement method."

In the comparative method, a value is arrived at by checking the prices obtained for similar properties that were sold recently. "Recently" is very important because of price fluctuation. It would be useless, for instance, to compare the price of your property with one that sold over a year ago; three months should be the limit. Professionals have free access to the sales figures, which makes their job a little easier than the one that you are about to undertake. You will have to indulge in a little subterfuge to make up for your lack of aids.

First, cruise your neighborhood, or neighborhoods of similar status to your own. Note the houses for sale that appear to be similar to your own. If your property is not on a corner lot, ignore those that are, because they tend to sell for a little less than those in the middle of the block.

When you have compiled a list of three of four, return home and phone the real estate offices concerned and try to obtain as much detail as possible. Your average "eager beaver" salesperson will be only too pleased to fill you in. The better-than-average realtor will talk you into having a look through the home. This is great, but whatever you do, go in your own car and meet at the site.

Most listing agents enjoy showing what they have for sale. After all, it shows their vendor some action and proves that they are on the job. Doubtless the realtor will phone you from time to time in an endeavor to introduce you to other likely properties, but you can always say you've changed your mind or stall with the "decided to wait until next year — I'll call you when I'm ready" bit. This may appear to be a dirty trick, but unfortunately, if you are out to make a buck you will probably have to be inconsiderate at times.

Now that you have ruthlessly obtained the information you require by finding and inspecting three homes that are very similar to your own, your list is as follows:

House A is listed at $62 900

House B is listed at $64 900

House C is listed at $63 500

Assuming that the above homes are priced expertly, at market value, it is usual in the real estate business to tack on 5% so that the seller can "come down a bit." Bearing this in mind, the selling prices of the above homes would be something like this:

House A — $60 000

House B — $62 500

House C — $61 500

It would seem, then, that your property would market at around the $60 000 level; therefore, your asking price should be $61 500. At this point we may as well figure out what the other house owners will eventually have in actual cash.

House A sold for $60 000. After commission, the owner will receive $56 400.

House B sold for $62 500. After commission, the owner will have $58 750.

House C sold for $61 500. After commission, $57 810. You, of course, will wind up with the full selling price, which proves the point: the effort is well worth while!

The second method of determining value is the replacement method, and this means exactly what it says. It's as if you wished to build your present home in its present location, at today's cost. First determine the square footage of the house (the length by the breadth), then check with a local builder as to his price for construction per square foot. You have measured the building and have arrived at a square footage of, say, 1 400. The builder has quoted you $25 per square foot, so you multiply 1 400 by $25 and reach a figure of $35 000. This figure would represent the cost of rebuilding your basic home. If you have any extras, such as a garage, fireplace, second bathroom, or whatever, add on another $5 000, giving you a total of $40 000. You know that the lot your house stands on is worth around $20 000, so you arrive back at the magical figure of $60 000. Incidentally, it is quite easy to ascertain the value of the land by searching the classified columns of your local newspaper. If you look long and hard enough you will find plenty of building lots for sale.

One last method of evaluation, which should only be used in a desperate situation, is to decide how much you need out of the house from a cash point of view. You know what you paid for it, you know how much is owing on it, and you know also that you require $30 000 to deposit on your new home. If your mortgage commitment is, say, $20 000, this would add up to $50 000 in total as a selling price. The danger in using this method of calculation is that you may be grossly under selling, and may be giving some lucky purchaser or speculator a big break at your expense. This is why, I repeat, only use this method for a quick sale, if the situation you are in is a desperate one, such as a new out-of-town job demanding immediate attention, or if the mortgage company is leaning on you and you have to get out from under.

And if you *are* in a tight situation, be wary of obliging "friends." I can recall knocking on the door of one grand old house — you know the type, circular driveway, grounds with lots of mature trees, gum wood trim, and all that. The owner had been trying unsuccessfully to sell privately (without the benefit of this book), and I hoped to be of service. The dear old lady who answered the door rejected my offer of assistance, as her neighbor down the road was going to buy the house from her — for no less than $30 000. At this, I was grateful for the fact that I did not have false teeth, because I am sure that I would have swallowed them. This home had to be in the $80 000 bracket. No doubt the dear old soul remembered that she and her husband paid only $15 000 for the home when they purchased it 40 years before, so a profit of $15 000 seemed handsome indeed. Naturally, she was quite dumbfounded when I informed her that the house should be on the market for around $85 000. Anyway, the upshot was that I listed the property and sold it for $82 500, out of which she gladly paid me my commission and still wound up over $50 000 richer than good neighbor Sam had intended her to be.

This anecdote, too, points out the dangers of under pricing. It is pointless going to all the trouble of selling the house yourself in order to save paying commission, if you are going to be worse off financially.

If these methods of pricing defeat you, then call in a professional appraiser. (The cost will not be exorbitant.) And when I say an appraiser, I mean just that. Do *not* call a real estate sales office, all you will get from the average salesperson is a figure intended to praise and flatter you in order to get a listing. Look through the Yellow Pages of your phone book for one of those long-established appraisal offices that every area has, one that specializes in residential estimating, and tell them you need a price for mortgaging purposes.

g. GIVE IT TIME
On many occasions I have called on private home sellers to solicit a listing, only to be told that they want to try it themselves for a couple of weeks. Believe me, this is no way to go about selling your own home; a couple of weeks is not

18

nearly enough. No real estate person, who, bear in mind, is a trained professional, would knock at your door and ask for a two-week listing. A realtor wants your home for just as long as he or she can get it; in fact, most multiple listing services demand at least a three-month term on their listing agreements.

We in the real estate business agree that there is a buyer somewhere for every piece of property, but that it normally takes time to find that person. During my career as a salesperson, I have had the good fortune on a number of occasions, to erect a "For Sale" sign on a front lawn and a "Sold" sign on the same lawn a couple of days later. Mark you, however, this is not the normal course of events. I wish it were. But, occasionally the right person will come along in a hurry, although usually the reverse is the case. I have known of houses that have been on the market for a year or more, but they do eventually sell. You are going to a lot of trouble to market your home, so do not give up too soon. If your price is right and the property is in good condition, it will sell. Do not expect speedy action if you are on a corner lot, or if you are located on a through road.

Have patience; everything comes to those who wait, so if you have not sold in the first week or so, don't rush out and give the sale to a realtor. In other words, do not be one of the private sellers who fail.

2

ADVERTISING

Well, at last you have arrived at the day when you are ready to advertise. You have been through the preparatory steps with care, you have made ready the house (and it is sparkling), you have all your facts and figures on hand, and you have decided on a sensible market value. So how do you advertise, and in what fashion?

Bearing in mind that the best things in life are free, let us first consider the methods that are not going to cost anything. Talk is cheap, so it is said, so tell everybody that you are selling. Word of mouth is a powerful agent, so talk about it, tell all your friends and neighbors, the cashier at the supermarket, the lady down at the laundromat, get the kids to spread the good word at school. You would be surprised at the number of sales that are made in this fashion. The chances of stumbling on to someone who knows someone who is looking for a home in your area are greater than you think. If you hear of any likely prospect, get them around to see the home. Remember that the house is all ready to be shown.

Another freebie is those supermarket notice boards, or the ones at the laundromat and the local gas station. Make it a family effort to print the advertisements and distribute them around the various locations. The notice-board advert should be written on what is no more than a postcard; no store or location would appreciate a streaming banner or a four-metre square poster.

Whether you are composing an advertisement for the press or for a notice board, the format should be the same. There are points that should stand out ahead of all others, and it is important to follow the guidelines as I set them out. The art of advertising is a highly skilled one, and while it is not my intention to turn you into a Madison Avenue expert, you do want to conduct a successful advertising campaign. So follow the rules.

The heading of an advertisement for anything should proclaim some outstanding feature, and in the case of your private house sale, the heading should be just that: "Private Sale," or "For Sale by Owner." These words have a magical quality, and suggest that there is a bargain to be had. The text of the message should begin with the next important point: location. To the average home buyer, the location of the property is of prime importance. Then, of course the price would be the next consideration. These three points should be followed by the style of the house, whether it be a brick bungalow, brick and frame side split, two-storey, or whatever. If you have aluminum siding, indicate this, because it is a good selling point. Indicate the number of bedrooms, size of lot, proximity to schools — all these are details that are well worth including. Do not be too wordy, stuff like "five years new," "hardwood under broadloom," "pegged floors," "hundred-amp wiring," are not of initial interest to your reader; these are some of the things to talk about when you meet. By the way, if you have one of those above-ground pools in the backyard, don't mention it. This could represent the unexpected little goodie that might swing the sale. Here is an example of the kind of layout that would be suitable for supermarket notice boards, or newspapers.

PRIVATE SALE

WEST BRIDLINGTON, asking $61 500, brick rancher, on a 60 x 120 lot, 3 bedrooms, 1 1/2 baths, finished family room, attached garage, close to schools, etc., owner transferred, early possession. Phone 000-0000.

Note, that in this example, the announcement is headed with the words "Private Sale," followed by the location and price, the most important points. If the lot is undersized, do not mention this in the ad, and if you have only one bathroom there's no need to point this out. Only include the selling points of the home; everybody knows you have a kitchen, so why waste money with unnecessary lineage? Remember, your advertisement should be designed to make the telephone ring.

If you are not in too big a hurry to sell (and you should have allowed yourself plenty of time, at least three months), let the free advertising sink in for a couple of weeks; you never know, you may not have to spend one penny on newspaper announcements.

Newspaper advertising need not be too costly. I have always favored what are known as word ads, or at the most, semi-display. My reasoning for this is not only an economic one, but I have always found that the response to this form of advertising is from people who are really looking for a home, and who are not just idly curious. Big advertisements with pictures are costly, they are more noticeable, and are seen by those folk who spend their weekends traipsing over other people's broadloom, but have no intention of buying. There are an awful lot of these people around, believe me.

The preceding example of an ad layout would be suitable for both notice boards and semi-display advertising, whereas a word advert would be something like this:
PRIVATE SALE. West Bridlington, asking $61 500, brick rancher, 60 x 120 lot, etc., etc.

Private "for sale" signs on the front lawn are very much a no-no. Very few sales are made from signs, the realtor's interest in your front lawn being not so much to sell your house, as to advertise the realtor's own name and company: "For Sale by GIGANTIC TRUST." At least you know that if it is a realtor's sign, anyone responding will have to call Gigantic Trust in order to view the home, and there is a certain comfort in the knowledge that this person will be accompanied by one of their representatives. Private signs, however, are an open invitation to any kook who happens to be cruising around the neighborhood, and believe me, there are an awful lot of them around. One last point before leaving the subject of advertising: *never* publish the address in either newspapers or on notice boards. The purpose of advertising is to make the telephone ring; if people know the address they tend to drive by, just to have a look at the outside. Very few homes are sold to "drive-byers," so make them phone you.

By the way, you will notice that I have advertised our $60 000 home for $61 500, and the reason for this is that everyone likes to haggle a bit. Nothing pleases a purchaser more than to be able to boast of getting the price down. Knowing that you are saving something like $3 000 in real estate commissions, the purchaser will offer something like $60 000 at the most, thinking: "That's $1 500 for the vendor and $1 500 for me. Live and let live, I always say."

3

HERE COME THE CUSTOMERS

a. ANSWERING THE TELEPHONE

You have probably been using a telephone for many long years and do not feel in need of any instruction in this area. However, the type of telephone technique that you are about to become involved in is somewhat different from the run-of-the-mill kittens or ten-speed bike, for sale, type of thing. You are now involved in big business, in selling something that's worth many thousands of dollars.

First, strict instructions should be handed out to the family that, if anyone calls about the house, the phone should immediately be handed over to Dad or Mom, or anyone equally authoritative. Never, but never, allow a youngster to gabble away, no matter how cute she sounds; people at the other end can become awfully frustrated and could very well hang up. So, parents, take charge, and during this period make sure that those teenagers of yours do not monopolize the wires; for a few weeks they are going to have to suffer the inconvenience of visiting their friends instead of phoning them. Let them know, however, that it is for a very good cause — your pocketbook.

At long last the great moment arrives, the telephone rings. Nobody makes a move, the family look at one another until Dad eventually drags himself out of his bean-bag chair, and totters over to the jangling instrument. It is strange that despite the fact that everyone has been working and waiting for this moment for a long time, now that the time has arrived all become very apprehensive, almost as if they were waiting in a dentist's outer office. However, Dad does answer, and will probably hear the following: "Do you have a house advertised in the *Daily Blurb?*"

Callers generally do not identify themselves for openers; there is always a reluctance on the part of people to say who they are, just in case what you have to offer is not what they are looking for, and being anonymous, they can hang up without further ado.

Anyway, you should respond to the opening statement with a friendly, "Yes, that is correct." Your caller will then continue with one or two leading questions, such as: "How old is the house?" or "How close is it to schools?" and, of course, having got all your facts and figures readily to hand, you will answer these questions with great alacrity. Be precise, do not be too pushy or wordy; in fact, make no comments other than replying. At this stage, you are trying to get them to view the home; this is the only way that you are going to sell it. You will never ever sell a home over a telelphone, so do not attempt to. Coming on too strong could frighten your prospect away.

After the initial quizzing, callers might decide, right then and there, that your house is not quite what they were looking for. If, however, they wish to make an appointment to view, arrange a day and time that is suitable to them. Remember, you are the seller, and if there is to be any inconveniences, it should be yours and not your prospects', so agree to their appointment, even if you have to change your plans. It is at this point that you should ask them for their name and telephone number. You hasten to explain that you need this, just in case any changes have to be made. If they readily supply you with this information, you probably have a live one; if not, then forget them, as your caller is more than likely to be a Nora Noseyneybor. The reasons that you require this information are threefold: first, you need to know who they are and roughly where they come from; second, you may have a genuine reason for cancelling, such as a sudden onset of German measles; and third, a reason which I will come to a little later on.

Your private-for-sale advertising will draw lots of calls from real estate agents; just inform them that you are planning on trying it yourself for a while. They may offer to show the property, claiming that they have a prospect. Make them understand that if they bring anyone through, your price is $60 000 firm, and that you want to clear this amount after expenses. Be polite in dealing with these people; remember they are only trying to make a living. Generally speaking, however, most of these agent calls are made to solicit the listing.

b. SHOW AND SELL

At long last you have reached the stage that you have been working and waiting for — that first showing. The house and the surrounds are as sharp as you can possibly make them, your clip board of facts and figures is conveniently at hand, and, by the way, it is good practice to have either a copy of your tax assessment or tax bill attached to these notes.

Just before your visitors are due to arrive, nip around and give the home a little of that "Lemon Pledge" treatment, check the bathrooms (young Joker sometimes forgets to flush the toilet), and tidy up in general. If it is an evening appointment, and it is most likely to be such, have subdued lighting on and very soft music playing. If you have a fireplace, and it is winter time, it is a good idea to have some logs crackling merrily away. However, if it is July and 90°, this is not a good idea, as your visitors will think that they have walked into some kind of nut house. Try to keep children and animals as inconspicuous as possible. Children are apt to blurt things out that you don't want advertised. I can recall one occasion while showing a property, when a 10-year-old announced in a loud voice that there was quicksand at the bottom of the garden! Of course, there was no such thing, but it certainly gave my clients a jolt, and despite my assurances to the contrary, they seemed to clutch their own youngster a little closer. Animals can be very distracting, especially a leaping, over-friendly pooch.

Generally speaking, it is good practice to have just one member of the family showing the guests through. Having the whole family, plus leaping dog trailing along, is very bad practice indeed. This situation always invites many voices to join in the conversation, all pointing out things they think the others have or will miss, resulting in very confused visitors.

Bear in mind that when you are trying to make a sale, you are walking a tightrope where the slightest little thing can tip the balance. Try to make your visitors feel as comfortable as possible by eliminating all the petty annoyances. Make them at least enjoy their visit and not glad to be "getting the heck out of there — those kids, that dog, my, my."

Remember, nobody would buy a house that they were glad to get out of. So, just one member of the family, please, and make sure that whoever it is has that clip board of answers. Do not forget that this step is just as important as the others that you have so diligently followed. You have worked hard for this moment, so do not blow it.

Something to bear in mind when showing your house is that a good realtor will always start with the most unattractive features of the house, and end the tour with the most attractive. This is not being deceiving, it is done for the obvious psychological effect. So if you have an unfinished basement, start with it. You could lead the way by saying, "Perhaps we should start at the bottom and work our way up, Mr. and Mrs. Jones." Or if the attic is just storage space; "Let us start at the top and work our way down." What I am trying to suggest here is that you do not hustle your folks into that Florida room that you are so justly proud of, and end the visit in that dank coal cellar. People have very short memories, and would certainly depart with unpleasant recollections, kicking the coal dust off their shoes. Always finish the tour in the most pleasant part of the home, whether it be the living room, family room, or at the bar in the recreation room.

Having completed the tour, invite them to have another look around this time on their own. The reasoning behind this is the fact that generally people will not speak their minds or criticize a home in front of the owner, which is quite understandable. After all, it is yours, and they know that you are very proud of it. So let them off on their own to mutter foul things in private. If your client declines the offer, the chances are that they are not very interested in your property.

After each tour, at least after each one that seemed successful, invite your guests to rest awhile. Remember, you have arrived back at the most attractive part of the house. Ask them to sit down, and when they are settled, ask them outright what they think of the home. If they are at all interested, they will ply you with a number of intelligent questions, for which you have all the answers ready. At this point they will raise any objections they may have: the color of the bedroom walls, for instance, and things of this nature. Of course, you must agree with them; do not argue, but offer to change or correct the particular defect. Anything smacking of a major operation, such as moving a garage back two metres, or widening the driveway to double its width, you would have to reject unless, of course, they are willing to tack the cost of these alterations on to the end price.

It is often effective to have some of the most important features of the house listed on a page that you can photocopy and give to interested people to take home with them. The kit of real estate forms published by Self-Counsel Press includes a "features sheet" of this nature (see Sample #1).

c. THE WISE BUYER

When buying a second-hand car, many people will kick the tires; whether they expect the car to sink to the ground in numerous bits and pieces, I will never know, but this seems to be about the extent of their knowledge of things mechanical. However, in house-buying the average person does know a little more. After all, he or she has always lived in a house of some kind and has had to fix things from time to time, so we assume from this that the average home buyer is somewhat more knowledgeable than the

SAMPLE #1
FEATURES SHEET

FEATURES SHEET

Owner's name _____ Ollie and Olivia Owner

Owner's address and phone number ____ 1111 High Way, Mortgage Heights, Anyprovince
                                                  999-0000

Asking price ____ $62 000

Address of residence for sale ____ Same as above

Legal description ____ Lot no. 99 Plan,no. 11111, Block 9

Lot size and characteristics ____ Frontage of 65 feet, depth of 120 feet
              Lot faces south, with lane in back

Size and nature of rooms

Kitchen ____ Pullman style, 18' x 6', built-in dishwasher

Living room ____ rectangular 30' x 20', 10' wide picture window on south

Dining room ____ 15' x 15' opening off of kitchen, built-in breakfront

Bathrooms ____ one full bath upstairs; one half bath off front hall

Bedrooms ____ 15' x 13' & double closet, 20' x 15' double closet

Basement ____ Laundry room 15' x 15'; finished family room with fireplace

Other rooms ____ and wet bar 30' x 50'

Taxes for 19 _79_ were: ____ $1150

Heating costs for _79_ were: ____ $600

Notable features are ____ Wall to wall carpeting throughout - 2 years old,
cream beige colour; New roof this year with additional

insulation; 5 blocks to elementary school; 2 blocks to

bus stop

Construction of house ____ Two story, frame construction with aluminum
siding

Existing mortgage ____ $40 000

Financing ____ Assumable mortgage at 11-3/4% on five-year term
              expiring September, 1981

INTERNATIONAL SELF-COUNSEL PRESS LTD.
306 West 25th Street
North Vancouver, British Columbia V7N 2G1
CAN-RSA-(3-1)78

automobile counterpart. It would be sound thinking, therefore, to consider some of the things that the "wise guy" will be looking for when inspecting your home.

There are the obvious faults, such as dampness in the basement and loose roof shingles, but you must also consider some of the less apparent matters. For instance, you have crossed your dining room floor a million times and heard the glasses jingling in the china cabinet, but do not let your prospect experience this. Either have the floor joists braced or move those jingling goblets apart. Another point of great interest to the cautious one is around the window frames and sills; he or she will be prodding and poking around there searching for damp rot. Check yours before showing, and if they are rotten, I am afraid you will have to replace them, or reduce your selling price to compensate. Bath tubs are another spot that usually come in for a great deal of attention. People, particularly the men, will examine the grouting and the tiles. Water and steam in the bathroom do cause havoc in the course of time, and poor or loose grouting that results from this, in particular around the top of the tub, can permit shower water to seep through into whatever is underneath. So check carefully. Electrical wiring and junction boxes will be thoroughly inspected and water faucets will be turned on to check the water pressure.

Then there is the search for sinkage cracks in the brickwork and foundations, loose floor boards, gaps under doors, banister railings that have a habit of popping out of the wall they are supposed to be attached to, and our snooper is bound to check these. No one wants a child or an aged mother falling down the stairs. Any rot of any kind, whether it be dry or damp, should be dealt with in one way or another; I leave it to your own conscience as to how you take care of it. These, then, are some of the things that the wise buyer will be looking at, so just make sure that they are taken care of before you start your showings.

d. QUALIFYING A PROSPECT

If your visitors gallop through the house as if they expected it to burst into flames at any minute, you can pretty well rule them out; they obviously did not even like the outside of it, and only came inside out of politeness because they had promised to do so. They will depart your domicile with "Very nice, we will be in touch." At the other end of the scale there are the over-enthusiastic ones who will ooh and aah over everything that they see, even the dog's dinner plate that they have just trodden into: "My, isn't that cute!" These types will leave the house with something like "Your home is just too lovely for words and we will most certainly let Uncle Fred know all about it." These are the over-polite ones, who on returning to their car will say "Yuck." Your best possibles are those who go through deliberately and slowly, and from whom you will hear snatches of conversation, such as "Wouldn't Janie like this room" or "I would put my sideboard there, and I think I would change the wallpaper in this room." These remarks, to anyone in the real estate business, are known as buyer signals, and people like this are "hot ones."

I hasten to add, however, that nothing is certain, you must still treat them with kid gloves; remember, you have nothing until it is down in black and white. These people do warrant special treatment, and to go a step further than in the last section, lead these likely ones back to the best room, arrange for them to sit facing the most attractive feature, maybe the view of the trees in the garden, or that fancy bar you have built in the basement. Offer them a cup of coffee or whatever, and then start to socialize a little; stop talking about the house, unless of course, they pose more questions. The main idea at this point is to try to get them to like you personally. In other words, you must sell yourself to them.

When they eventually stand up to go, they are quite likely to say: "We would like to sleep on this and get back in touch with you." Thank them very much for coming, and escort them to the door. If on peeping through the curtains (and you will) you note that they are a long while driving off, then you have probably found a real live one. However, do not rush out at this point and tell your neighbors that you sold your house, or for that matter phone Aunt Agatha. You have not sold yet, and will not have done so, until you have a signed contract in your hot little hands.

One advantage that a realtor has over the average "do-it-yourselfer" is the fact that he or she can follow up clients, and does so by calling them the next day, and sounding them out by asking them direct questions, such as whether they think the location is suitable, or whether they like the style of the house, and if there are no objections, urging them to come to the real estate office and write up an offer. "We are getting a lot of action here, and I don't think it will be on the market very much longer," the realtor will add. On the other hand, if during the previous night's "pillow talk," the clients have come up with some reservations, the realtor will suggest that they take a second look, and if they agree to do so, he or she is more than likely to sign them up.

The average private seller is unable to do this, but since by the time you have finished reading this book you will no longer be the average type, *you* can. This is the third reason why you asked them for their name and phone number on that first contact.

This, then, will be the procedure to follow. After supper on the evening following the showing, give your prospects a call. "Hello there, Mr. Doe. This is Jack Hoe, just thought I would give you a call regarding our house. You seemed very interested in it last night, and as we are getting a lot of enquiries about it (which would probably be true during the first advertising campaign), I felt that you should be the first to know." The answer that you will receive will be one of three. "I am sorry, but we have talked it over, and realize that with the kind of down payment we have, the mortgage payments would be more than we could handle," or "Yes, we are still very interested, but there are one or two things we were not too sure about." At this point you should emulate the good realtor and invite them back for a second look. If they accept the invitation, then, like the salesperson, you have a live one.

The third, and, of course, the most gratifying of all, is "Yes, we would like to buy your house." With this type of response, you have almost done it.

But not quite. There is still this matter of getting it down in writing. It is probably at this stage that a lot of private sales fall through. The vendor, quite certain of the sale, allows the prospective purchaser to arrange the documentation, the purchaser doesn't hurry, and in the meanwhile sees a home that he or she likes much better. Result, one lost transaction.

You should, instead, get your prospects to come back to the house, and note here that I use the plural. In the case of married couples, one signature is no good without the other. You are now about to show them how to save money themselves. I hasten to add here that you should not say so at this point; in other words, do not jump the gun. Merely suggest that they visit to talk the whole thing over. You are now about to "get it in writing." This leads into the real estate contract, called an agreement of purchase and sale, an interim agreement, or an offer to purchase depending where you live. To understand this, you must know something about the law of contracts.

4

SIGN ON THE DOTTED LINE

a. THE LAW OF CONTRACT

Before attempting to draw up any kind of agreement, it is imperative to know something about contracts and the laws governing them. If you are able to discuss aspects of a contract in an intelligent fashion, this should inspire a certain confidence in your prospect. "Boy, does that guy know what he is talking about!" Remember, when you are trying to sell the house yourself you must be able to supply the same kind of service that a real estate salesperson can, with the same kind of authority. So, once your clients have decided to buy, do not let them off with the "I will go to see my lawyer" bit; as I have already mentioned, you could quite easily lose them. Get it down on paper first, then let them go to see their lawyer.

In brief, a contract is an agreement between two or more people, to do, or not to do, some specific thing. It can be oral or in writing; however, insofar as real estate transactions are concerned, the law is that they must be in writing. Allow me to repeat this: *it must be in writing*. You simply have not sold your house if someone agrees to purchase it, and offers to shake hands on it, no matter how firm the grip.

b. THE INGREDIENTS OF A CONTRACT

There are certain elements to a binding real estate contract that you should know. They are as follows. .

1. Mutual agreement

This is the first stage, and the one in which both parties have mutually agreed to the terms of the contract. For example: price, method of financing, what extras go with the property, the closing date of the transaction. In other words, a complete meeting of the minds.

2. Consideration

You cannot offer to do something for someone without expecting something of value in return, and vice versa. The consideration in a real estate transaction is normally the deposit with the offer. This deposit also represents a sign of good faith. If there were no cash commitment involved, the jokers of this world could run around putting offers in on properties willy nilly, and create a chaotic situation.

3. Capacity

There are certain people who cannot be held to a contract whether it be written or oral. Anyone intoxicated or under the influence of drugs at the time of signing cannot be bound, so if your purchaser shows signs of having been into the sauce or suds or whatever, suggest that the paper work be left until the next day.

The mentally incompetent cannot be held responsible for their signature. I can recall selling a house to a young lady, who after signing the contract and having it accepted, suggested that I call her brother, who was also in the market for a house. I duly telephoned said brother with opening remarks something like this: "Hello Lou, I have just sold your sister Sue a house on Dunagain Drive." At this point brother Lou cut me off with a very deep sigh and replied, "Oh my God, not again." Apparently, this young lady, who had recently been paroled from a mental institution, made a practice of running around buying property that she could not afford and, of course, could not be held responsible for.

A third party lacking the capacity to sign a contract is one who is under the age of majority. In some areas this is 21 years, and in others, 18 years of age. This varies from place to place, and you should know what this is for your particular situation.

4. Intention

The offer and the acceptance thereof must be genuine. If a person is induced to sign, or there is any fraud, duress, or flagrant misrepresentation involved, any contract would be null and void. For instance, if you assured your prospect that there was a gold mine two metres under the garden, and they were stupid enough to believe you and sign a contract as the result of this belief, you just would not have a contract when the truth was discovered. In addition, in this extreme case, you would be guilty of fraudulent misrepresentation.

5. Lawful object

A contract must be a lawful one, it cannot be one that binds a person to commit fraud or civil wrong. By the way, under the Lord's Day Act in Canada, one cannot sign real estate documents on Sunday, or on any legal statutory holiday. So bear this in mind, and make sure that your signing date is not on the Sabbath or on a legal holiday such as Christmas Day. All copies of a contract must be signed as an original; in other words, do not sign through carbon paper. In addition, each signature must have the date alongside it in the signer's writing.

c. UNDERSTANDING THE DOCUMENT

The document that you will sign is known in the real estate profession as the "offer," as initially this is exactly what it is. It is the form used by the purchaser to make the offer. If and when it is accepted by the vendor, it then becomes an agreement of purchase and sale — a binding contract.

This form is fairly standard throughout North America, although it may vary in style and title from place to place: for instance, in Alberta, it is called the offer to purchase and interim agreement; in British Columbia, the interim agreement; and in Ontario, the agreement of purchase and sale.

Self-Counsel Press publishes a kit of forms which not only includes the required documents for your area, but a list of some of the clauses that you may have to use in the course of your transaction. These kits are available in most good book stores. If they are not obtainable in your area, you may purchase other pre-printed forms at most stationery stores.

The form is usually sold in multiple copies because all parties to a transaction of this nature must, by law, receive a copy of the document they have signed, for instance, a man and wife purchaser, a man and wife vendor, and of course, the two lawyers who will eventually be involved in the transaction.

The three provincial forms that I have mentioned are very similar in content with only minor differences. We will look at each one in turn, starting with Alberta's offer to purchase and interim agreement. (See Sample #2.)

Section 1 on the front page of the form is fairly straightforward, beginning with the name of the purchaser, the municipal address and legal description of the property, the date of the actual inspection, the name of the vendor, the offering price (written in full followed by figures), and lastly, the deposit with the offer (the valuable consideration).

Section 2 deals with the method of payment. If it is all cash, the appropriate box should be checked. If it is not, describe the manner in which the balance is to be paid, either expressed as a down payment with a mortgage to be taken back by the vendor, or by arranging new financing.

Section 3 is where you would insert any conditions that are in the transaction such as the sale of the purchaser's house or raising new financing, or whatever. The list of possible clauses included in the Self-Counsel Press kit would be invaluable at this point.

SAMPLE #2
OFFER TO PURCHASE
(ALBERTA)

ALBERTA

Offer to Purchase and Interim Agreement

1. The undersigned __Ollie and Olivia Offre__,

Legal and residential description

herein called the Purchaser, having inspected the real property described as __222 Oil Lane,__ __Calgary, Lot 22, Block 23, Plan 2043 H.F. Windsor__ _____ on the __4th__ day of __June__, 19 __80__

herein agrees to and with __Sam and Sue Seller__,

herein called the Vendor, to purchase the said inspected real property at the price of __ninety__ __thousand__ Dollars ($ __90 000.00__) of which the sum of __five__ __thousand__ Dollars ($ __5 000.00__) the Purchaser pays to and is received by __Sol Solisitor__ _____ as a deposit on account of the purchase price, on the following terms and conditions.

Check proper box. If ALL CASH then there is no need to put in any more information.

2. The purchase price is payable as: ☒ All cash on completion; or ☐ $_____ Cash

on completion with the balance as follows: _____

Here insert any terms concerning the Vendor taking back a second mortgage or an Agreement for Sale. It is unnecessary to insert the terms of a mortgage between the Purchaser and a third party who is not the Vendor here.

_____
_____
_____
_____

Here the Purchaser will insert terms such as those concerning a building inspection or the sale of his own residence for certain terms.

3. This offer is made subject to the following conditions: __These terms are for__ __the benefit of the Purchaser and may be waived by the__ __Purchaser alone.__ __(a) Subject to the Purchaser arranging a first mortgage__ __within 30 days from the acceptance of this offer in the__ __amount of $50 000.00 at 16% per annum__

4. The balance of cash is to be paid by __September 15__, 19 __80__ and the sale completed by __September 15__, 19 __80__.

5. A conveyance by way of a deed, transfer of land, mortgage or agreement for sale on the terms set out herein shall be delivered to the Purchaser or to the Purchaser's solicitor on or before the date set for completion.

6. The Purchaser will assume and pay taxes, water and sewer rates and continuing charges, and all adjustments will be made as of __September 15__, 19 __80__.

7. Provided the sale is completed, the Purchaser is to have vacant possession of the property (subject to existing tenancies) at __one__ o'clock __p.__.m. on __September 15__, 19 __80__.

8. All buildings and chattels included in the sale shall be and remain at the risk of the Vendor, until the date of adjustments, and all insurance policies and the proceeds thereof shall be held in trust for the parties as their interests may appear.

INTERNATIONAL SELF-COUNSEL PRESS LTD.
306 West 25th Street
North Vancouver, British Columbia V7N 2G1
CAN-RSA-ALTA(1-1)78

SAMPLE #2 — Continued

9. The Purchaser accepts title subject to restrictive covenants, statutory building schemes, reservations and exceptions in the original grant from the Crown, easements in favour of utilities, public authorities and adjacent lands, buildings, zoning and other municipal or government restrictions and also subject to existing tenancies and the Purchaser is satisfied as to the legality of any suites on the property.

10. The purchase price includes any buildings, improvements, fixtures, appurtenances and attachments and all television antennae, blinds, awnings, screen doors and windows, storm windows, curtain rods, tracks and valances, fixed mirrors, fixed carpeting, electric plumbing and heating fixtures and appurtenances and attachments thereto present on the date of inspection, except the following:

Here Vendor lists any fixtures that are not going to be sold with the property.

Family room bar

11. There are no representations, warranties, guarantees, promises or agreements other than those contained in this agreement and words importing the singular, masculine or neuter shall mean and include the plural, feminine or body corporate wherever the context or the parties hereto so require.

12. The Vendor shall bear all costs of discharging any mortgage or other encumbrance that is not herein assumed by the Purchaser. The Purchaser will bear all costs of the conveyance and, if applicable, any costs relating to arranging a mortgage.

13. This offer, when accepted, shall constitute a binding contract of purchase and sale and time shall be of the essence.

14. The Vendor represents and warrants to the Purchaser that:
   (a) he is not now, nor will be 60 days after the possession date, a non-resident of Canada within the meaning of the Income Tax Act of Canada, and
   (b) he is not the agent or trustee for anyone with an interest in this property who is, or will be 60 days after the possession date, a non-resident of Canada within the meaning of the Income Tax Act of Canada.

15. This offer shall be held open for acceptance by the Vendor until __Five__ o'clock
__p__.m. on __June 6__, 19 __80__.

16. If the offer is not accepted by the Vendor within this time, the offer shall become null and void and the deposit shall be returned to the Purchaser without interest.

DATED at __Calgary__, this __5th__ day of __June__, 19 __80__.

SIGNED in the presence of:

__Wilma Witness__
Witness

__Ollie Offer__
Signature of Purchaser

__Bus driver__
Occupation

__Olivia Offer__
Signature of Co-Purchaser

__999-1111__; __6 High St, Calgary__
Phone   Address

Acceptance

I, the undersigned, the Vendor of the above described property, hereby accept the above offer together with all conditions contained therein. I further agree to and with the Purchaser to duly complete the sale on the terms and conditions of the above offer and should I fail to do so, the Purchaser may (at his option) cancel the agreement and withdraw his deposit, or take whatever remedies he, the Purchaser, may have at law.

DATED at __Calgary__, this __5th__ day of __June__, 19 __80__.

SIGNED in the presence of:

__Willie Witness__

__Sam Seller__
Signature of Vendor

__111-9999__   __222 Oil Lane, Calgary__
Phone   Address

__Sue Seller__
Signature of Co-Vendor or Vendor's Spouse

INTERNATIONAL SELF-COUNSEL PRESS LTD.
306 West 25th Street
North Vancouver, British Columbia V7N 2G1
CAN-RSA-ALTA(1-2)78

40

SAMPLE #2 — Continued

ALBERTA

INFORMATION FOR YOUR LAWYERS

Vendor's full name _Sam and Sue Seller_

Address _222 Oil Lane, Calgary_ Telephone number _111-9999_

Vendor's wife's name and address if different ____

Address ____

Vendor's lawyer _Sol Solister_

Address _555 Legalise Lane, Calgary_

Purchaser's full name _Ollie Offre_

Address _6 High Street Calgary_ Telephone number _999-1111_

Co-Purchaser's name ____

Deed or Transfer of Land to be made to _Ollie and Olivia Offre_

Dated _____ 19___

TO _____

**Offer to Purchase
and
Interim Agreement**

INTERNATIONAL SELF-COUNSEL PRESS LTD
306 West 25th Street
North Vancouver, British Columbia V7N 2G1
CAN-ISA-ALTA(-3)78

41

Sections 4, 6, and 7 show the dates on which the transaction should be completed, and usually these dates are the same, although the date in section 4 could be a day ahead of the others.

Section 5 is the area that will be handled by your lawyer.

Section 8 is an important one to consider. Up to and until the time that your purchaser takes possession of your property, it is your responsibility; therefore, if you plan on vacating prior to the closing date, make sure that someone is looking after the house.

Section 9 is the one where the purchaser agrees to accept title, the covenants, and the easements that go with it.

Section 10 is where any fixtures that do not remain with the property must be noted. For example, maybe the chandelier in the dining room is a family heirloom and will be replaced. It is also important to include the fact that certain fixtures may be rental items such as water heaters or oil burners. If you fail to note this, you could very well wind up paying these rentals for the rest of your life.

The next section that you will be concerned with is section 15. This is the irrevocable date, or the date up until which the offer is good (usually this is midnight of the day that the offer is made, as the purchaser is quite anxious to know whether or not he or she has bought a house).

Last but not least is the signature section. By the way, in passing, it would be a good idea to include the name and address of the purchaser's lawyer in the section on "Information for Lawyers."

In British Columbia, the form is known as the interim agreement (see Sample #3). The first page is similar to the offer that has already been described. Section 8, however, includes a specific time (e.g., 12 o'clock noon) after which the vendor is no longer responsible for the property. The irrevocable date and the signatures follow at the bottom.

Ontario's agreement of purchase and sale is likewise similar (see Sample #4). There is one important difference which should be noted in particular: if the property being sold is registered in the name of one owner, for example, a man — or his wife — singularly, in order to protect the interests of the excluded spouse, the following must be included in the agreement:

> "The undersigned spouse of the vendor hereby consents to the disposition herein pursuant to the provisions of the Family Law Reform Act, 1978, as the same may be amended from time to time. In the consideration of the sum of One Dollar ($1.00), the receipt of which from the purchaser is hereby acknowledged, the undersigned spouse of the vendor hereby agrees that he/she will execute all necessary or incidental documents to give full force and effect to the sale evidenced herein" _____ (followed by a space for a signature).

The purchaser must then give the non-involved spouse one dollar for which he or she signs in the space provided.

SAMPLE #3
INTERIM AGREEMENT
(BRITISH COLUMBIA)

BRITISH COLUMBIA

Interim Agreement

1. The undersigned ___Betty Byer___

Legal description and residential address.

herein called the Purchaser, having inspected the real property described as __747 Boeing Ave,__ __Riceland, Block 23, District 456, Plan 7890'__

____ on the __6th__ day of __October__ , 19 __80__ .

herein agrees to and with ___Sally Sail___ .

herein called the Vendor, to purchase the said real property at the price of __Seventy__ __Thousand__ Dollars ($__70 000.00__) of which the sum of __Two__ __Thousand__ Dollars ($__2 000.00__) the Purchaser pays to and is received by ____ __Sally Sail__ ____ as a deposit on account of the purchase price, on the following terms and conditions.

Check proper box. If "All cash," then there is no need to put in any more information here. If otherwise, insert terms of Vendor's Agreement for Sale or mortgage to be assumed.

2. The purchase price is payable as: ☒ All cash on completion; or ☐ $ _____ Cash on completion with the balance as follows: ____

____

____

____

____

Here Purchaser or Vendor can put terms regarding the sale of his own home, tenancies, etc.

3. This offer is made subject to the following conditions: __These terms are__ __for the benefit of the Purchaser and may be waived by the__ __Purchaser alone:__

__(a) The dwelling on the real property being purchased has been__ __constructed in accordance with and presently complies__ __with all relevant municipal, provincial, and federal__ __requirements.__

__(b) The heating system, plumbing system, electrical system__ __are not in need of repair.__

4. The balance of cash is to be paid by __November 27__ , 19 __80__ , and the sale completed by __November 27__ , 19 __80__ .

5. Provided the sale is completed, the Purchaser is to have vacant possession of the property, (subject to existing tenancies) at __12 noon__ o'clock __p.__ .m. on __November 28__ , 19 __80__ .

6. Purchaser will assume and pay taxes, water and sewer rates and continuing charges, and adjustments shall be made as of __12 noon, November 28, 1980__

Delivery is accomplished by the Vendor signing the documents prepared by the Purchaser's solicitor.

7. A conveyance by way of a deed, mortgage or agreement for sale on the terms set out herein and in registerable form shall be delivered to the Purchaser or the Purchaser's solicitor on or before the date set for completion.

INTERNATIONAL SELF-COUNSEL PRESS LTD
306 West 25th Street
North Vancouver, British Columbia V7N 2G1
CAN-RSA-BC11-1/78

44

SAMPLE #3 — Continued

8. The property shall be at the risk of the Vendor until 12 o'clock noon on the adjustment date and thereafter at the risk of the Purchaser and in the event that buildings or improvements thereon are destroyed or substantially damaged prior to that time, either party may at his option cancel this agreement and all monies paid under this agreement shall be returned.

9. Title is subject to restrictive covenants, statutory building schemes, reservations and exceptions contained in the original grant from the Crown, easements in favour of utilities, public authorities, and adjacent land, building, zoning and other municipal or governmental restrictions, and also to be subject to existing tenancies and the Purchaser is satisfied as to the legality of any suites on the property.

List any fixtures that will not be sold to the Purchaser with the house.

10. The purchase price includes any buildings, improvements, fixtures, appurtenances and attachments and all television antennae, blinds, awnings, screen doors and windows, storm windows, curtain rods, tracks and valances, fixed mirrors, fixed carpeting, electric plumbing, and heating fixtures and appurtenances and attachments thereto, present on the date of inspection, except the following:

Chandelier dining room , Dishwasher
Front porch swing

11. The Vendor is to clear the title of all charges, encumbrances and judgments not assumed herein by the Purchaser, unless the parties arrange for deduction and discharge of same from the sale proceeds. Purchaser will pay all costs of conveyancing and arranging any mortgage, if applicable.

12. There are no representations, warranties, guarantees, promises or agreements other than those contained in this agreement, and words importing the singular, masculine and neuter shall mean and include the plural, feminine or body corporate wherever the context or parties to this agreement require.

13. The offer, when accepted, shall constitute a binding contract of purchase and sale and time shall be of the essence.

14. The Vendor represents and warrants to the Purchaser that:
(a) he is not now, nor will be 60 days after the possession date, a non-resident of Canada within the meaning of the Income Tax Act of Canada.
(b) he is not the agent or trustee for anyone with an interest in this property who is or will be 60 days after the possession date a non-resident of Canada within the meaning of the Income Tax Act of Canada.

15. This offer shall be held open for acceptance by the Vendor until _eight_ o'clock _p_.m. on _October 7_ , 19 _80_ .

16. If the offer is not accepted by the Vendor within this time, the offer shall become null and void and the deposit shall be returned to the Purchaser without interest.

Offer

I hereby agree and offer to purchase the property at the price and on the terms and conditions herein set out.

Purchaser _Betty Byer_   Purchaser _____
Occupation _Fashion designer_   Occupation _____
Dated _October 6, 1980_

Acceptance

I hereby accept the above offer on the terms and conditions contained therein.

Vendor _Sally Saul_   Vendor _____
Occupation _Boat builder_   Occupation _____
Dated _October 7, 1980_

INTERNATIONAL SELF-COUNSEL PRESS LTD
306 West 25th Street
North Vancouver, British Columbia V7N 2G1
CAN-RSA-BC11-2178

45

SAMPLE #3 — Continued

INFORMATION FOR YOUR LAWYERS

Vendor's full name __Sally Sail__

Address __747 Boeing Avenue, Riceland, B.C.__

Vendor's wife's name and address if different __N/A__

Address __N/A__

Vendor's lawyer __Barry Barrister__

Address __100 Torte Lane, Riceland, B.C.__

Telephone number __666-1111__

Purchaser's full name __Betty Byer__

Address __200 Renter's Row, Riceland__

Co-Purchaser's name _____

Telephone number __999-2222__

Deed or Transfer of Land to be made to __Betty Byer__

SAMPLE #4
AGREEMENT OF PURCHASE AND SALE
(ONTARIO)

ONTARIO

Agreement of Purchase and Sale

1. The undersigned __Peter Purchaser__ _____.

Put in residential address and legal description.

herein called the Purchaser, having inspected the real property described as __123 Any Street,__ __on the north side of Any Street, City of Hamilton, Lot 32,__ __Plan 10572__ _____ on the __2nd__ day of __September__, 19 __80__

herein agrees to and with __Vera Vendor__ _____

herein called the Vendor, to purchase the said real property at the price of __Sixty-two__ __Thousand__ Dollars ($ __62 000.00__) payable as ☐ all of which the sum of __One__ __Thousand__ Dollars ($ __1 000.00__) the Purchaser pays to and is received by _____

__Tom Trustee__ _____ as a deposit on account of the purchase price.

1A. The purchase price is payable as follows:☒All Cash on completion; or☐_____ Cash

on completion with the balance as follows: _____

_____

Here put any terms concerning the Vendor's agreement to take a second mortgage or an agreement for sale from the Purchaser. Also put terms such as the sale being subject to building inspection, or the sale of the Purchaser's present home here.

2. This offer is made subject to the following conditions: __These terms are for the__ __benefit of the Purchaser and may be waived by the Purchaser__ __alone.__ __(a) Subject to the Purchaser selling his home at 222 Lake__ __Drive, Hamilton, for $60 000.00 with completion date__ __to be on or before December 15, 1980.__

3. The Purchaser accepts title free and clear of encumbrances, except restrictive covenants, existing tenancies, reservations and exceptions in the original grant from the Crown, and municipal requirements, including building and zoning by-laws. Provided the title is good and free from all encumbrances (except those assumed by the Purchaser as aforesaid), the Purchaser is not to call for the production of any title deed, abstract or other evidence of title except such as are in the possession of the Vendor. This agreement shall be conditional upon the Vendor, at his own expense complying with the provisions of the Planning Act.

4. The Purchaser is allowed __30__ days from the date of acceptance of this offer to examine the title at his own expense. If a valid objection to title is made in writing to the Vendor within that time and the Vendor is unable or unwilling to remove the objection and the Purchaser is unwilling to waive his objection, then this agreement shall be null and void and the deposit shall be returned to the Purchaser without interest.

5. The balance of the purchase price is to be tendered in cash or negotiable certified cheque by __December 31__, 19 __80__ and the sale completed by __December 31__, 19 __80__.

6. A conveyance by way of a deed, transfer of land, mortgage or agreement for sale on the terms set out herein shall be delivered to the Purchaser or the Purchaser's solicitor on the date fixed for completion.

7. The Purchaser will assume and pay all taxes, rates, local improvements, assignments and continuing charges and all adjustments shall be made as of __December 31, 1980__.

8. The Purchaser is to have vacant possession of the property (subject to existing tenancies) at __eight__ o'clock __p.__ m. on __December 31__, 19 __80__.

9. The Purchaser will bear all costs of the conveyance and, if applicable, any costs related to arranging a mortgage, and the Vendor will bear all costs of clearing title.

10. Pending completion of sale, the Vendor will hold all insurance policies and the proceeds thereof in trust for the parties as their interests may appear. The property shall be at the risk of the Purchaser from and including the adjustment date.

Here Vendor lists any fixture that is not going to be sold with the house

11. The purchase price includes any buildings, improvements, fixtures, appurtenances and attachments and all television antennae, blinds, awnings, screen doors and windows, storm windows, curtain rods, tracks and valances, fixed mirrors, fixed carpeting, electric, plumbing and heating fixtures

and appurtenances and attachments thereto, except the following: _Wood curtain rods_
in living, dining, and family rooms

12. There are no representations, warranties, guarantees, promises or agreements other than those contained herein, and words importing the singular, masculine, or neuter shall mean and include the plural, feminine or body corporate where the context or the parties hereto require.

13. This offer, when accepted, shall constitute a binding contract of purchase and sale and time shall be of the essence.

14. The Vendor represents and warrants to the purchaser that:
(a) he is not now, nor will be 60 days after the possession date, a non-resident of Canada within the meaning of the Income Tax Act of Canada, and
(b) he is not the agent or trustee for anyone with an interest in this property who is, or will be 60 days after the possession date, a non-resident of Canada within the meaning of the Income Tax Act of Canada.

15. This offer shall be held open for acceptance by the Vendor until _ten_ o'clock
_p_.m. on _September 3_, 19 _80_ and upon acceptance by the signing of a copy of this offer by the Vendor there shall be a binding agreement of sale and purchase on the terms and conditions herein set forth.

16. If the offer is not accepted by the Vendor within this time, this offer shall become null and void and the deposit shall be returned to the Purchaser without interest.

Offer

I hereby offer and agree to purchase the property at the price and on the terms and conditions herein set out.

DATED at _Hamilton_, this _2nd_ day of _September_, A.D. 19 _80_.

SIGNED, SEALED AND DELIVERED
in the presence of:

Ima Witness

IN WITNESS whereof I have hereunto set
my hand and seal,

Peter Purchaser
Purchaser

Purchaser

Acceptance

I hereby accept the above offer and terms and conditions.

DATED at _Hamilton_, this _3rd_ day of _September_, A.D. 19 _80_.

SIGNED, SEALED AND DELIVERED
in the presence of:

Ura Witness

IN WITNESS whereof I have hereunto set
my hand and seal,

Van Vendor
Vendor

Vendor

INTERNATIONAL SELF-COUNSEL PRESS LTD.
306 West 25th Street
North Vancouver, British Columbia V7N 2G1
CAN-RSA-ONT(1)-8/79

SAMPLE #4 — Continued

ONTARIO

INFORMATION FOR LAWYERS

Vendor's full name and address _Vera Vendor_

Telephone number _533-4444_

Wife's full name and address: _____

Vendor's lawyer _Tom Trustee_

Purchaser's full name and address _Peter Purchaser_
456 Nowhere Rd, Hamilton Telephone number _222-3333_

Co-Purchaser's name _____

Purchaser's lawyer _Laura Lawyer_

Title to be issued to _Peter Purchaser_

Dated

**Agreement
of
Purchase and Sale**

TO

19

In other provinces and in places where the Self-Counsel kit is unavailable, you will have to contend with the more cumbersome forms used by realtors and often sold at stationery stores.

Once again, let's take it step by step. First, study the preamble. It will be something like this.

THE UNDERSIGNED _____ herein called the purchaser, having inspected the real property, hereby agrees to and with _____ herein called the vendor.

I think that you will agree that this is self-explanatory, and is a mere filling in of the names of the parties involved in the blank spaces. Following this, some standard forms have a space for the agent's name through whom the transaction is being made. As we are not dealing through an agent but selling privately, leave this space blank.

Following this, you will find:

TO PURCHASE ALL AND SINGULAR THE PREMISES ON THE _____ SIDE OF _____ IN THE _____ OF _____ AND KNOWN AS _____ .

Let us consider this section for a moment. The premises being purchased are on the north, south, east or west side of such and such a street, in the county, town or whatever of so and so, and known as Municipal Number (street number). Having a frontage of so many feet more or less, by a depth of so many feet more or less, and being lot number six, plan M5, or however this is described on your tax form.

Following this there will be:

AT THE PRICE OF _____

and in this space, the price should be set out in full, e.g., SIXTY THOUSAND DOLLARS, followed by the figures $60 000, (as you would write a cheque). Under the price you will find:

PAYABLE BY CHEQUE OR CASH _____

This refers to the deposit with the offer. Going back to the law of contract, this is the "valuable consideration."

The final part of the preamble will continue with:

TO THE AGENT FOR THE VENDOR AS A DEPOSIT TO BE HELD BY SUCH AGENT IN TRUST PENDING COMPLETION OR OTHER TERMINATION OF THE AGREEMENT AND TO BE CREDITED ON ACCOUNT OF PURCHASE MONEY ON CLOSING, AND THE PURCHASER AGREES TO _____.

Delete the words, THE AGENT FOR and the words BY SUCH AGENT. Any deletions of this nature should be initialled by all signing parties.

The body of the offer is the big blank space in the middle, and this is where all the clauses and conditions are inserted (see section d. for a detailed discussion).

The third and final part, you will note, contains most of the small print, and has the spaces for the various signatures and dates, and so on. It is always claimed, and in most cases quite rightly so, that one should be familiar with the small print on a contract. With a real estate document of this nature, however, you will find that the wording is standard, there are no tricks or traps, the original having been drawn up by the legal profession, in some cases merely repeating in legal terminology what you have written in the body of the document. However, it will be as well to go over some of this wording, not only to set your mind at rest, but just in case your prospective purchaser asks any questions.

On the standard form the small print will start something like this:

> PROVIDED THAT THE TITLE IS GOOD AND FREE FROM ALL ENCUMBRANCES EXCEPT AS AFORESAID AND EXCEPT AS TO ANY REGISTERED RESTRICTIONS OR COVENANTS THAT RUN WITH THE LAND, PROVING THAT SUCH ARE COMPLIED WITH.

In basic English this could be interpreted to read as follows: the contract is O.K., provided you are aware of any liens, or whatever on the property. EXCEPT AS AFORESAID refers to the matters that you have inserted in the body of the offer, and the REGISTERED RESTRICTIONS OR COVENANTS THAT RUN WITH THE LAND merely points out the fact that all property has certain restrictions upon it. For example, if the house is designated a single-family dwelling, then it must be used as such and not for multi-family or commercial use.

To continue: THE PURCHASER TO ACCEPT ALL THE USUAL PUBLIC UTILITY EASEMENTS. Most properties have some kind of easement on them, whether it be the telephone company or local utilities, and this clause is inserted to acquaint the purchaser with the fact that these people have the right to enter said lands to service their equipment, and so on.

To continue:

> THE PURCHASER IS TO BE ALLOWED _____ DAYS FROM THE DATE OF ACCEPTANCE HEREOF TO EXAMINE THE TITLE AT HIS OWN EXPENSE. IF WITHIN THAT TIME, ANY VALID OBJECTION TO TITLE IS MADE IN WRITING TO THE VENDOR WHICH THE VENDOR SHALL BE UNABLE OR UNWILLING TO REMOVE, THIS AGREEMENT SHALL BE NULL AND VOID AND THE PURCHASERS' DEPOSIT RETURNED IN FULL.

The time allowed for the purchaser to examine the title is that time that it takes the lawyer to check out the documents at the land titles or registry office — usually 15 days. If the purchasers' lawyer found something on the title which clouded it, and you, the vendor, are unwilling or unable to clear same, then the deal falls through. (See Glossary for an explanation of "cloud on title." Fortunately, once the contract has been signed by both parties, lawyers do most of the rest of the work and you do not have to worry about things like finding the cloud on the title.)

> THIS OFFER WHEN ACCEPTED SHALL CONSTITUTE A BINDING CONTRACT OF PURCHASE AND SALE, AND TIME SHALL IN ALL RESPECTS BE OF THE ESSENCE HEREOF.

In other words, this is it, times and dates must be adhered to, unless any mutual agreement to changes is made.

The next point of interest is the irrevocable date, and this section reads thus:

> THIS OFFER SHALL BE IRREVOCABLE BY THE PURCHASER UP UNTIL AND INCLUDING THE _____ DAY OF _____ 19 ____.

This is the date until which your purchasers' offer is good; any time after this, if not accepted, it becomes null and void. There will be mention of this point again a little later on, so skip that for now and let us continue with the fine print.

> THIS TRANSACTION OF PURCHASE AND SALE IS TO BE COMPLETED ON OR BEFORE THE _____ DAY OF _____ 19 ____.

This is the closing date, the day on which you will be forsaking the old homestead.

Under the purchasers' signatures there are instructions regarding the payment of commissions. Leave this blank, as there are none to be paid.

d. DRAWING UP THE AGREEMENT

In this section, we will be dealing with the various clauses that you may be faced with, and these will be entered in the body of the agreement, that section which has the big blank space. I will start at the beginning with a typical preamble, and fill it in, as you will eventually have to. The printed matter on the form I will show in upper case or capitals, and the inserts in lower case, so that you will be able to identify that which is already there, and that which you will have to add.

THE UNDERSIGNED George Henry Doe and Mary Joyce Doe HEREIN CALLED THE PURCHASERS. HAVING INSPECTED THE REAL PROPERTY AGREES TO AND WITH Frederick Charles Hoe and Jane Hoe THROUGH _____ AGENTS FOR THE VENDOR. TO PURCHASE ALL AND SINGULAR THE PREMISES ON THE east SIDE OF Kent Avenue IN THE COUNTY OF Dude AND KNOWN AS municipal number 20, lot 20, plan M6, having a frontage of sixty feet more or less by a depth of one hundred and twenty feet more or less HEREIN CALLED THE REAL PROPERTY. AT THE PRICE OF sixty thousand dollars ($60 000.00) PAYABLE BY CHEQUE OR CASH one thousand dollars ($1 000.00) TO THE AGENT FOR THE VENDOR TO BE HELD BY SUCH AGENT IN TRUST PENDING COMPLETION OR OTHER TERMINATION OF THIS AGREEMENT AND TO BE CREDITED ON ACCOUNT OF PURCHASE MONEY ON CLOSING, AND THE PURCHASER AGREES TO _____

This is the end of the preamble, and these are the points to remember when filling it in. First, ensure that all names of the parties concerned are written out in full. Second, when describing the size of the lot, make sure that the words "more or less" follow the dimensions. These are inserted so that there can be no argument over a discrepancy in inches, and I do mean inches. Third, ex out the following words, "THE AGENT FOR" and further along the words "BY SUCH AGENT". Finally, while still on the preamble, it is good thinking to have your purchaser make the deposit cheque out to your lawyer's trust account, just in case something goes wrong and the money has to be refunded. It can be very embarrassing if you have purchased drapes for your new home using the $1 000 deposit, only to have the deal fall through, and you have to come up with this amount in a hurry.

This then is the preamble and is the easy part, so if you feel up to it, continue with the body — the nitty-gritty of the offer.

The preamble ends with the words, AND THE PURCHASER AGREES TO _____ followed by lots of blank space. This is where you insert all the terms and conditions concerning the purchase. In the first place, let's assume that your offer is a straightforward cash one, and that the house is selling for $60 000 with a deposit of $1 000. This then would be the format.

> AND THE PURCHASER AGREES TO Pay a further sum of fifty-nine thousand dollars ($59 000.00), by cash or certified cheque to the vendor on date of closing subject to the usual adjustments.

The words "subject to the usual adjustments" refer to any real estate taxes that are paid in advance, fire insurance premiums, if these are to continue, and any other minor payments of this nature. However, as these will all be computed by your lawyer on closing day, do not worry. I merely point this out so that you will know what it is all about, as your purchaser is bound to ask.

To finish this part of the offer, add the following:

> The vendor agrees to discharge any mortgages or liens now on the property, at his own expense.

Whether there are any encumbrances of this nature on the property or not, this sentence should be included.

The straightforward cash offer is, generally speaking, about as rare as hen's teeth, and the examples that follow are the ones you will more likely be faced with. Let us next consider a mortgage "take-over" situation, and for this purchase let's assume that there is an existing assumable mortgage on the property of $40 000. This then, would be your wording, bearing in mind that you have a $1 000 deposit.

AND THE PURCHASER AGREES TO pay a further sum of nineteen thousand dollars ($19 000.00) by cash or certified cheque subject to the usual adjustments to the vendor on date of closing.

The purchaser further agrees to assume an existing first mortgage now on the property of approximately forty thousand dollars ($40 000.00) bearing interest at the rate of 10% per annum, calculated semi-annually, not in advance, and repayable in blended monthly instalments of four hundred dollars ($400.00) to include both interest and principal and to run for a term of eight years from date of closing.

The figures that I quote here are, of course, just examples, but it is easy enough to transpose these into the actual amounts that apply to your mortgage, by taking the figures off your mortgage document. Before going to the trouble of inserting this mortgage take-over clause, make sure that your loan is a transferable one; some are not. If you cannot find it on the actual document (some of them are difficult to sort out), then call your mortgage company. If you learn that it is not transferable, then you run into the next condition which is a "subject clause," whereby the offer is conditional upon the purchaser arranging new financing. Using the same figures that you used before, your wording would be as follows:

AND THE PURCHASER AGREES TO pay a further sum of nineteen thousand dollars ($19 000.00) by cash or certified cheque subject to the usual adjustments to the vendor on date of closing.

This offer is conditional upon the purchaser arranging a new first mortgage in the amount of forty thousand dollars ($40 000.00) bearing interest at the rate of not more than 10% per annum calculated semi-annually, not in advance and repayable in blended monthly instalments of four hundred dollars ($400.00) to include both interest and principal. This mortgage to run for a term of five years from the date of closing. Fourteen days are to be allowed to

arrange said mortgage from the date of the acceptance of
this offer, and failure to do so renders this offer null and
void and the purchasers' deposit is to be returned in full
without interest or deduction. The vendor agrees to
discharge any mortgages now on the property at his own
expense.

Regarding the above condition, there are a couple of
points you should be careful of. Ensure that the mortgage
applied for is a realistic one and at whatever the going rate
happens to be (which changes almost weekly these days). It
would be quite useless to make the offer subject to the
purchaser arranging a new mortgage at 3%, even if Uncle
Fred has promised them a low interest loan. Insert the
going rate, and then if Uncle fails to come across, your offer
is still a valid one. Another point to be careful of: make sure
that the mortgage applied for is a sensible one — it's no
good applying for a $59 000 loan on a $60 000 house. Be
very careful about things like this; it would be a crying
shame to have done all this work and have it all come to
naught. You could assure your party, however, that
although you are entering an amount of say 15%, they are
not bound to accept anything higher, and if they are able to
arrange cheaper private money, that is their good luck.

The third type of condition that you may become
involved with is the offer that is conditional upon the sale
of the purchasers' own home. If your people have a house
to sell, then more than likely the basic offer will be of the
cash variety, or at least they will have sufficient funds to
assume the existing mortgage. The body of the offer, then,
should be set out either as the straightforward cash offer,
or as assuming the existing mortgage, so instead of
inserting the mortgage-raising clause, you would use the
following terminology:

This offer is conditional upon the purchasers selling
their property known as (*the address of the house*) on or before
such and such a date (*allow at least two months*). Failing this
renders the offer null and void and the purchasers' deposit
returned to them in full without interest or deduction.

To protect yourself, and avoid tying the property up for this length of time in what may be an exercise in complete frustration, you must add the following rider, which is termed an escape clause, and will allow you to get out from under if your purchasers' property is a tough one to sell. This should read as follows:

> Providing that the vendor may continue to offer his property for sale, and if receiving an acceptable offer shall give the purchaser 72 hours' notice in writing to clear said condition, Sundays and statutory holidays not included. Failure to do so renders this offer null and void and the purchasers' deposit returned in full without interest or deductions.

The value of this escape clause is quite obvious because if another purchaser pops up with a firm offer, you will not have to keep him or her dangling for two months, just 72 hours. You will note that throughout this chapter, I repeat the terminology. I do this deliberately, in order to make you more than familiar with it, as when you get to the offer stage, I want you to do it right.

The third section of the document is that which contains the small print and as this was discussed in detail in section c. we will move on to the blank spaces that you have to fill in.

The first one that you come to follows the words: THE PURCHASER IS TO BE ALLOWED _____ DAYS. This is the time that the purchasers' lawyer will need to search title, so put the number 15 in this spot. Moving on down, you will see THIS TRANSACTION OF THE PURCHASE AND SALE IS TO BE COMPLETED ON OR BEFORE THE _____ DAY OF _____ 19 ____ , and in here you put the actual closing date.

The next blank spot to be filled in is after the sentence dealing with the chattels and fixtures, which goes something like this:

ANY STORM OR SCREEN SASH OR DOORS, WATER HEATER AND PRESENT HEATING EQUIPMENT,

ELECTRICAL AND PLUMBING FIXTURES, T.V. ANTENNA AND ALL OTHER PERMANENT FIXTURES USUAL TO THE BUILDING, OTHER THAN THE CHATTELS SHALL REMAIN WITH THE PROPERTY UNLESS OTHERWISE PROVIDED AS FOLLOWS:

In the blank space that follows should be noted any rental items, such as the hot water heater or furnace or water softener. It is sufficient to say that the hot water heater, or whatever, is a rental item. The final blank space in the small print is where the irrevocable date goes, this being the date up to which the offer is good. If you and your prospect are writing up the offer there and then (and I sincerely hope that you are), it would be sufficient to have that day's date inserted here. If, however, your couple wants to see their lawyer before signing, then make the date a couple of days hence.

At this point, remove the carbon paper, if any, in preparation for signing; all signatures must be original, and there are, perhaps, six copies to be signed. Just above the section for the signatures, you will see something like this:

DATED AT _____ THIS _____ DAY OF _____
19 _____.

After the word "dated at," it is important to insert here the actual place of signing, not the location of the house, so if you happen to be up north in the cottage, or down south in Florida, make sure that the name of that particular place is entered here. Underneath this section, you will see the spaces for the actual signatures, and after each name, the date of signing should once again be inserted, e.g., John Doe 10/10/1980.

Well, that is it, you have achieved what you once considered impossible. Before you reach this stage, however, there are still some more things to be learned. So let us plow on.

e. TENANCY

In real estate transactions, there are two types of tenancy when property is jointly owned. One is known as "joint tenancy," and the other "tenancy in common." The difference is described in the following paragraphs.

Joint tenancy is that form of registration usually adopted in a man and wife purchase, and is one whereby both names are put on the deed. The advantage is that if one of the signing parties should die, that half of the property automatically reverts to the surviving partner. Naturally, this is the most common-sense arrangement for married couples.

Tenancy in common is the form of agreement in which if one of the parties should die, his or her half of the home goes to his or her estate, and not to the survivor. This generally means that the property involved would have to be sold to satisfy the demands of the estate. Tenancy in common is usual in the case of a person and a partner doing some real estate dabbling on the side, maybe investing in some income property, or whatever. This does ensure that the spouse of the deceased gets his or her share of the spoils. Tenancy in common would also be used if there were a number of purchasers involved, unless, of course, they were all family.

If, when drawing up the offer, only one of the joint tenants involved in the transaction is present, it is all right for that one person to sign, or to make the offer without the other joint tenant being present; the offer would still be a binding one. It is only necessary for the joint tenancy to be noted on the deed. I hasten to add at this point that the acceptance of the offer by the vendor must have both signatures if the property is owned jointly.

Tenancy in common, on the other hand, is a business arrangement and both parties should sign any offer to purchase property, unless, of course, there is some form of written agreement between them.

f. FIXTURES AND CHATTELS

When disposing of real estate it is important to know the difference between chattels and fixtures. Many a law suit has resulted from a lack of this knowledge, and many a deal fallen through, and as you have gone this far in preparing for the sale and worked so hard, don't leave any stone unturned in ensuring a successful conclusion.

Fixtures or fittings, as they are sometimes termed, are those items which cannot be removed from a piece of property without leaving some form of damage. For instance, the bath tub would be considered a fixture. Other examples would be fitted broadloom, light fixtures, drapery tracks or built-in book shelves, to name a few. In some cases where, say, a certain light fitting or whatever has some form of sentimental value or is a priceless antique, and the owner desires to remove it, this should be noted in the body of the agreement after the monetary details. Do not leave it as a verbal agreement, but put it down in writing. It is all very well to tell your clients when walking through the house, that you intend removing the light fixture in the dining room. They may agree at the time, and forget what you have said by the time moving day rolls around. It comes as a bit of a shock to them, when they take over, to find that the chandelier they had admired so much is gone and has been replaced by a hole in the ceiling. If, however, it was specifically stated in the agreement, then they cannot come back at you. I cannot stress this point enough; in word-of-mouth agreements, people can have very short memories and you could find yourself in all kinds of difficulties.

While on the subject of light fittings (and these are the things most often involved in disputes), we in the real estate business are highly trained in making a contract as watertight as possible, at the same time protecting ourselves and the vendor, and we would note right on the offer that the lighting fixture in the dining room or wherever is to be replaced by a suitable fixture. Note that we say "will be replaced"; never, ever, leave a hole in the ceiling. In this way the point is spelled out in black and white, and cannot be disputed. This would apply, of course, to any type of fixture that you wished to remove. The golden rule is *put it down in writing;* this keeps everybody happy. By the way, it is common courtesy to repair any damage you may do when removing fixtures; plaster up those holes and remove any nails or brackets.

Chattels are those things which can be removed without causing any damage, and, of course, include your furniture, kitchen appliances such as refrigerator, stove, and things of this nature. Very often, however, such things as refrigerators and stoves are included in the sale, in which case this too should be noted in the offer, with one proviso. If your agreement is one which is conditional upon raising a fairly high mortgage, do not include chattels in the document, because as you will learn in the chapter on mortgages, they can have an effect on the amount of the loan. In this case, it would be as well to make an arrangement on the side with regard to any extras.

You may think that I am belaboring small points in the above paragraph, but believe me, they are not as small as you may think. I have done some research on the reasons for unsuccessful private home sales, and I have learned that it was something as insignificant as the removal of a humidifier from a furnace, or the tearing out of some cheap wooden shelves, that blew their deal. So learn from the mistakes of others.

5

MORTGAGES

Further to my efforts to give you all the advantages enjoyed by the real estate professional, this chapter on mortgages is a must, and should be studied with great care. Arranging financing is, or could be, a stumbling block to the successful conclusion of your transaction, and it is up to you to be able to advise your purchaser, especially if they are first-time home buyers and have never before been involved with this type of financing.

A mortgage is a sum of money loaned, with real property as collateral, or to put it in its official jargon, "A conveyance of property to a lender, as security for payment of a debt, with a right of redemption."

a. FINANCING

There are various sources of mortgage money — banks, trust companies, private individuals, and lawyers who very often have client money to invest. If, however, you are trying to set up a mortgage for your purchaser (and you should help if they request), your first approach should be your bank manager — as a rule, a good source of money, or information. Another good person to talk to is your lawyer. Bear in mind, however, that all you can do for your client is to set the wheels in motion, and having done so it is then up to him or her to get together with the lender. In section e. of this chapter you will find a schedule of mortgage repayments ranging from 10% up to 20%, showing the monthly payments required to carry them. This is included to assist you in writing up your agreement, as the more specific you can be, the sounder your transaction.

There are two terms used in reference to mortgages with which you should be familiar. The first is "amortization," a term which refers to the number of years that it would take to discharge or pay back a mortgage, making equal monthly payments. This amortization is normally 25 years, and you will note that the mortgage repayment schedule is computed on the basis of 25 years, this being the most practical length of time.

The second word that you will come across is "term." This refers to the length of time for which the money is on loan. Nowadays, this period is usually five years. Naturally, no mortgage could be discharged in this short space of time, as the monthly payments would be astronomical, so in this case, at the end of five years, you have to refinance, although the existing lender would quite likely give an extension at the going rate, that is, if the loan is in good standing, and the monthly payments have been made regularly.

b. QUALIFICATION FOR A MORTGAGE

Qualification requirements may vary from place to place, but usually the monthly payments must not exceed 30% of the joint incomes of the borrowers. It is more than likely that you will find this figure is the one for most localities; however, local requirements can be ascertained from your bank or mortgage company. If the mortgage amount applied for is, say, $40 000 at 10%, the monthly payments as shown in our repayment schedule are $357.80, or roughly $4 294.00 per year. Therefore, our borrowers would have to have a joint income of at least $14 500.00 per year. (Good luck finding a mortgage at 10% anywhere these days!)

c. TYPES OF MORTGAGES

The first mortgage is known as the legal mortgage, and a second mortgage as an equity loan, that is a loan based on how much equity an owner has in a property. The equity is the value of the property over and above the amount of the first mortgage. Both loans are registered against the property, of course, although the first takes preference over the second. The situation could arise where, in order to facilitate the sale of your house, you have to take back a small second mortgage.

There is nothing wrong in this, although some caution is advised. For instance, if you were selling your house for $60 000, and the existing first or the proposed new first mortgage is $40 000, it would be a dangerous exercise to take back a second mortgage of say, $18 000 on a down payment of $2 000. By all means, if you do not require the cash, accept a mortgage of $10 000 with a down payment to match. This would be reasonably safe, as anyone putting out that amount of cash is not likely to default. If they did, however, you are very well covered. There is one safe method of selling your house where a low down payment is involved, and that is by an Agreement for Sale. Please do not confuse this with an agreement of purchase and sale.

An Agreement for Sale is one in which the purchaser has a small down payment and the vendor takes back the whole balance, including the first mortgage on an agreement. For instance, the price of the house is, say, $60 000, the first mortgage is $40 000, leaving a balance of $20 000. The purchaser has a down payment of $3 000, which leaves an amount of $17 000 to be accounted for and this would be registered against the property as a second mortgage, bearing interest at a percentage point above the interest on the first mortgage. On taking over the house, the buyer is then responsible for making the payments for *both* mortgages to the vendor, who in turn continues to make the monthly payments on the first mortgage as before.

As a form of compensation for this chore, the vendor would be receiving an interest rate of a percentage point above that of the first mortgage for the whole amount. In other words, if the first mortgage was $40 000 at 9% per annum, the second of $17 000 would bear an interest rate of 10%. Thus, the overall interest would be 10% and the vendor would be receiving an extra percentage on the $40 000, or about $400 per year as recompense for handling the money.

Another advantage in this form of arrangement is that if there is any delinquency in payments, the defaulter can be given a month's notice and the rigmarole that has to be gone through when a normal mortgage falls foul is thus avoided. The purchaser in an Agreement for Sale does not receive a deed to the property and, although he or she is technically buying the house and has the right of redemption, has very little equity in it, and is just a little better than a tenant.

When taking back a second mortgage, it is a good practice to make the term the same as the first mortgage; for example, if the first is due in three years, make the due date of the second the same; thus the term on your second mortgage would be three years instead of the normal five.

If your reason for selling is to retire to the country or to Florida, your own property is a sound investment. If your purchaser has a good down payment, at least 15% of the value or selling price, you would be quite safe in taking back the balance as a first mortgage. In this event it would be a good policy to offer the money at a percentage point less than the going rate. This would certainly facilitate the sale! Remember, you are not in the mortgage lending business, and you would still be getting a satisfactory return on your investment, plus the fact that you have very good security. If you merely put your money in the bank, they will most certainly lend it out in mortgages or such, and make money out of your money. Make sure that you do not give too long a term, however — no more than five years; in this way, the balance is due and payable at that time, and then you can decide whether or not you would want to continue the arrangement, or buy Bell Telephone stock, or whatever.

d. MORTGAGE CONDITIONS

Mortgages do contain certain privileges, and anything that is to the advantage of the borrower is termed a privilege. Some, for instance, are fully open, which means that they can be paid off at any time without notice or bonus. This usually applies to most private monies. For instance, if you take back any kind of mortgage you would have these prepayment privileges on your document. Mortgage companies which, after all, are in the business of lending money, are not quite as easygoing as this, and would require a penalty of at least three months' interest if a borrower wished to discharge a loan. Some companies will, however, grant the privilege of paying off 10% of the principal sum each year on the anniversary (you could almost call it an anniversary present). Some mortgages are completely closed, if not for the whole term, for at least three years of it. Many of the various clauses that are entered on to a mortgage document are negotiable between lender and borrower at the time that the arrangement is being made, and if you are unhappy with the conditions, argue the point. Remember, these people are quite eager to put their money out, and are just as anxious to do business with you as you are with them.

There are a couple of things I want you to bear in mind. First, all this talk of mortgage documents and privileges should not be of any consequence as far as you, the seller, are concerned. Your responsibility goes no further than making sure that all the mortgage details are included in the body of the offer. Forget the privileges and details of this kind; all you need to concern yourself with is the amount of the mortgage, the percentage, the repayments and the term. Insofar as the actual mortgage document is concerned and the registering of same, this is not your worry, since the purchaser's lawyer will take care of all this.

Second, if you are taking back a first mortgage, a second mortgage or even an Agreement for Sale, check out the credit rating of your clients, ask them to supply you with references and, above all, a letter from their employers as to the amount of their earnings during the previous year. If you have any difficulty doing this, ask your lawyer. He or she is well able to take care of this.

e. REPAYMENT SCHEDULE

To assist you in drawing up the contract with your purchasers, I have prepared a loan repayment schedule. It is important for the information entered on the contract to be correct.

The principal amount of the mortgage is in the left hand column of the schedule, and at the top of the page you will see the various interest rates, which range from a low of 10% to a high of 20%. To find the monthly payments for any given amount with any interest rate, simply run your finger along the column until you are under the desired rate and there you have the monthly payment, which includes both interest and principal. For instance, if the principal sum if $20 000 with an interest rate of 10%, you will note that where the two columns meet, you have a monthly payment of $178.90. All the payments in this schedule are based on 25 years amortization, this being the most practical. Remember, the term, especially in these high interest rate days, should not be for more than 5 years.

MORTGAGE REPAYMENT SCHEDULE

Amount	10%	10½%	11%	11¼%	11½%	12%	12¼%
$	$	$	$	$	$	$	$
10,000	89.45	92.84	96.26	97.98	99.71	103.19	104.95
11,000	98.40	102.12	105.88	107.78	109.68	113.51	115.44
12,000	107.34	111.40	115.51	117.58	119.65	123.83	125.94
13,000	116.29	120.69	125.13	127.37	129.62	134.15	136.43
14,000	125.23	129.97	134.76	137.17	139.59	144.47	146.92
15,000	134.18	139.25	144.38	146.97	149.56	154.79	157.42
16,000	143.12	148.54	154.01	156.77	159.53	165.11	167.91
17,000	152.07	157.82	163.63	166.56	169.51	175.43	178.41
18,000	161.01	167.10	173.26	176.36	179.48	185.75	188.90
19,000	169.96	176.39	182.89	186.16	189.45	196.07	199.40
20,000	178.90	185.67	192.51	195,96	199.42	206.38	209.89
21,000	187.85	194.95	202.14	205.75	209.39	216.70	220.38
22,000	196.79	204.24	211.76	215.55	219.36	227.02	230.88
23,000	205.74	213.52	221.39	225.35	229.33	237.34	241.37
24,000	214.68	222.80	231.01	235.15	239.30	247.66	251.87
25,000	223.63	232.09	240.64	244.94	249.27	257.98	262.36
26,000	232.57	241.37	250.26	254.74	259.24	268.30	272.86
27,000	241.52	250.65	259.89	264.54	269.21	278.62	283.35
28,000	250.46	259.94	269.51	274.34	279.18	288.94	293.84
29,000	259.41	269.22	279.14	284.13	289.15	299.26	304.34
30,000	268.35	278.50	288.76	293.93	299.12	309.57	314.83
31,000	277.30	287.79	298.39	303.73	309.09	318.89	325.33
32,000	286.24	297.07	308.01	313.53	319.06	330.21	335.82
33,000	295.19	306.35	317.64	323.32	329.03	340.53	346.32
34,000	304.13	315.64	327.26	333.12	339.01	350.85	356.81
35,000	313.08	324.92	336.89	342.92	348.98	361.17	367.30
36,000	322.02	334.20	346.52	352.72	358.95	371.49	377.80
37,000	330.97	343.49	356.14	362.51	368.92	381.81	388.29
38,000	339.91	352.77	365.77	372.31	378.89	392.13	398.79
39,000	348.86	362.05	375.39	382.11	388.86	402.45	409.28
40,000	357.80	371.34	385.02	391.91	398.83	412.76	419.78
41,000	366.74	380.62	394.64	401.70	408.80	423.08	430.27
42,000	375.69	389.90	404.27	411.50	418.77	433.40	440.76
43,000	384.63	399.19	413.89	421.30	428.74	443.72	451.26
44,000	393.58	408.47	423.52	431.10	438.71	454.04	461.75
45,000	402.52	417.75	433.14	440.89	448.68	464.36	472.25
50,000	447.25	464.17	481.27	489.88	498.54	515.95	524.72

Amount	12½%	12¾%	13%	13¼%	13½%	13¾%	14%
$	$	$	$	$	$	$	$
10,000	106.71	108.47	110.25	112.02	113.81	115.60	117.39
11,000	117.38	119.32	121.27	123.23	125.19	127.16	129.13
12,000	128.05	130.17	132.29	134.43	136.57	138.72	140.87
13,000	138.72	141.01	143.32	145.63	147.95	150.28	152.61
14,000	149.39	151.86	154.34	156.83	159.33	161.83	164.35
15,000	160.06	162.71	165.37	168.03	170.71	173.39	176.09
16,000	170.73	173.55	176.39	179.24	182.09	184.95	187.83
17,000	181.40	184.40	187.41	190.44	193.47	196.51	199.56
18,000	192.07	195.25	198.44	201.64	204.85	208.07	211.30
19,000	202.74	206.09	209.46	212.84	216.23	219.63	223.04
20,000	213.41	216.94	220.49	224.04	227.61	231.19	234.78
21,000	224.08	227.79	231.51	235.25	238.99	242.75	246.52
22,000	234.75	238.64	242.53	246.45	250.37	254.31	258.26
23,000	245.42	249.48	253.56	257.65	261.75	265.87	270.00
24,000	256.09	260.33	264.58	268.85	273.13	277.43	281.74
25,000	266.76	271.18	275.61	280.05	284.51	288.99	293.47
26,000	277.43	282.02	286.63	291.25	295.89	300.55	305.21
27,000	288.10	292.87	297.66	302.46	307.27	312.11	316.95
28,000	298.77	303.72	308.68	313.66	318.65	323.66	328.69
29,000	309.44	314.56	319.70	324.86	330.03	335.22	340.43
30,000	320.11	325.41	330.73	336.06	341.41	346.78	352.17
31,000	330.78	336.26	341.75	347.26	352.80	358.34	363.91
32,000	341.45	347.10	352.78	358.47	364.18	369.90	375.65
33,000	352.12	357.95	363.80	369.67	375.56	381.46	387.38
34,000	362.79	368.80	374.82	380.87	386.94	393.02	399.12
35,000	373.46	379.64	385.85	392.07	398.32	404.58	410.86
36,000	384.13	390.49	396.87	403.27	409.70	416.14	422.60
37,000	394.80	401.34	407.90	414.48	421.08	427.70	434.34
38,000	405.47	412.18	418.92	425.68	432.46	439.26	446.08
39,000	416.14	423.03	429.94	436.88	443.84	450.82	457.82
40,000	426.81	433.88	440.97	448.08	455.22	462.38	469.56
42,000	437.48	444.73	451.99	459.28	466.60	473.94	481.29
42,000	448.15	455.57	463.02	470.49	477.98	485.49	493.03
43,000	458.82	466.42	474.04	481.69	489.36	497.05	504.77
44,000	469.49	477.27	485.06	492.89	500.74	508.61	516.51
45,000	480.17	488.11	496.09	504.09	512.12	520.17	528.25
50,000	533.52	542.35	551.21	560.10	569.02	577.97	586.94

Amount	14¼%	14½%	14¾%	15%	15¼%	15½%	15¾%
$	$	$	$	$	$	$	$
10,000	119.19	121.00	122.81	124.62	126.44	128.26	130.08
11,000	131.11	133.10	135.09	137.08	139.08	141.08	143.09
12,000	143.03	145.20	147.37	149.54	151.72	153.91	156.10
13,000	154.95	157.29	159.65	162.00	164.37	166.73	169.11
14,000	166.87	169.39	171.93	174.47	177.01	179.56	182.11
15,000	178.79	181.49	184.21	186.93	189.65	192.39	195.12
16,000	190.70	193.59	196.49	199.39	202.30	205.21	208.13
17,000	202.62	205.69	208.77	211.85	214.94	218.04	221.14
18,000	214.54	217.79	221.05	224.31	227.58	230.86	234.15
19,000	226.46	229.89	233.33	236.77	240.23	243.69	247.15
20,000	238.38	241.99	245.61	249.23	252.87	256.51	260.16
21,000	250.30	254.09	257.89	261.70	265.51	269.34	273.17
22,000	262.22	266.19	270.17	274.16	278.16	282.16	286.18
23,000	274.14	278.29	282.45	286.62	290.80	294.99	299.19
24,000	286.05	290.39	294.73	299.08	303.44	307.81	312.19
25,000	297.97	302.49	307.01	311.54	316.09	320.64	325.20
26,000	309.89	314.58	319.29	324.00	328.73	333.46	338.21
27,000	321.81	326.68	331.57	336.46	341.37	346.29	351.22
28,000	333.73	338.78	343.85	348.93	354.01	359.11	364.22
29,000	345.65	350.88	356.13	361.39	366.66	371.94	377.23
30,000	357.57	362.98	368.41	373.85	379.30	384.77	390.24
31,000	369.49	375.08	380.69	386.31	391.94	397.59	403.25
32,000	381.40	387.18	392.97	398.77	404.59	410.42	416.26
33,000	393.32	399.28	405.25	411.23	417.23	423.24	429.26
34,000	405.24	411.38	417.53	423.69	429.87	436.07	442.27
35,000	417.16	423.48	429.81	436.16	442.52	448.89	455.28
36,000	429.08	435.58	442.09	448.62	455.16	461.72	468.29
37,000	441.00	447.86	454.37	461.08	467.80	474.54	481.30
38,000	452.92	459.77	466.65	473.54	480.45	487.37	494.30
39,000	464.84	471.87	478.93	486.00	493.09	500.19	507.31
40,000	476.75	483.97	491.21	498.46	505.73	513.02	520.32
41,000	488.67	496.07	503.49	510.92	518.38	525.84	533.33
42,000	500.59	508.17	515.77	523.39	531.02	538.67	546.33
43,000	512.51	520.27	528.05	535.85	543.66	551.49	559.34
44,000	524.43	532.37	540.33	548.31	556.31	564.32	572.35
45,000	536.35	544.47	552.61	560.77	568.95	577.15	585.36
50,000	595.94	604.97	614.01	623.08	632.17	641.27	650.40

Amount	16%	16½%	17%	17½%	18%	19%	20%
$	$	$	$	$	$	$	$
10,000	131.91	135.58	139.26	142.95	146.64	156.06	161.50
11,000	145.10	149.14	153.18	157.24	161.31	169.47	177.65
12,000	158.29	162.69	167.11	171.53	175.97	184.87	193.80
13,000	171.48	176.25	181.03	185.83	190.63	200.28	209.95
14,000	184.67	189.81	194.96	200.12	205.30	215.68	226.10
15,000	197.87	203.37	208.88	214.42	219.96	231.09	242.25
16,000	211.06	216.92	222.81	228.71	234.63	246.49	258.40
17,000	224.25	230.48	236.73	243.00	249.29	261.90	274.55
18,000	237.44	244.04	250.66	257.30	263.95	277.30	290.69
19,000	250.63	257.59	264.58	271.59	278.62	292.71	306.84
20,000	263.82	271.15	278.51	285.89	293.28	308.12	322.99
21,000	277.01	284.71	292.43	300.18	307.94	323.52	339.14
22,000	290.20	298.27	306.36	314.47	322.61	338.93	355.29
23,000	303.39	311.82	320.28	328.77	337.27	354.33	371.44
24,000	316.58	325.38	334.21	343.06	351.94	369.74	387.59
25,000	329.77	338.94	348.13	357.36	366.60	385.14	403.74
26,000	342.96	352.50	362.06	371.65	381.26	400.55	419.89
27,000	356.15	366.05	375.99	385.94	395.93	415.95	436.04
28,000	369.34	379.61	389.91	400.24	410.59	431.36	452.19
29,000	382.54	393.17	403.84	414.53	425.26	446.76	468.34
30,000	395.73	406.73	417.76	428.83	439.92	462.17	484.49
31,000	408.92	420.28	431.69	443.12	454.58	477.58	500.64
32,000	422.11	433.84	445.61	457.41	469.25	492.98	516.79
33,000	435.30	447.40	459.54	471.71	483.91	508.39	532.94
34,000	448.49	460.96	473.46	486.00	498.57	523.79	549.09
35,000	461.68	474.51	487.39	500.30	513.24	539.20	565.24
36,000	474.87	488.07	501.31	514.59	527.90	554.60	581.38
37,000	488.06	501.63	515.24	528.88	542.57	570.01	597.53
38,000	501.25	515.18	529.16	543.18	557.23	585.41	613.68
39,000	514.44	528.74	543.09	557.47	571.89	600.82	629.83
40,000	527.63	542.30	557.01	471.77	586.56	616.23	645.98
41,000	540.82	555.86	570.94	586.06	601.22	631.63	662.13
42,000	554.01	569.41	584.86	600.36	615.88	647.04	678.28
43,000	567.21	582.97	598.79	614.65	630.55	662.44	694.43
44,000	580.40	596.54	612.71	628.94	645.21	677.85	710.58
45,000	593.59	610.09	626.64	643.24	659.88	693.25	726.73
50,000	659.54	677.87	696.26	714.71	733.19	770.28	807.48

6

LEGAL FEES AND COSTS

There are certain legal fees involved in the purchase and sale of real estate. These may vary from place to place, but they are basically as follows.

In the purchase of property, the legal charges are somewhat higher than those charged for selling, owing to the fact that the lawyer has to search the title. He or she generally does this during the period allowed for on the agreement, but then has to return to the registry office on or about closing day to look over what is known as the "Day Book," the day-to-day record of anything that may have affected the property since the original search was conducted. Generally speaking, the purchaser's lawyer has a good deal more responsibility than the one who is acting for the vendor.

The vendor's lawyer handles the monetary side of the transaction, discharging liens and unrequired mortgages, and paying any expenses involved in the sale. He or she has little to do apart from transferring the funds, unless there are any complications.

Remember, however, that whether you are buying or selling a property, lawyers' charges are not fixed. So if you think that you are being taken to the cleaners by your particular lawyer, shop around; they are all out for business and you will find them quite willing to talk price.

Some of the costs other than actual legal fees that can be involved are as follows:

(a) Land transfer tax

(b) Sheriff's certificate

(c) Registering the deed or mortgage

(d) Tax certificate

(e) Title search

Your particular locality may have a few more goodies of this nature to throw at you, but basically these are the main charges you will be faced with.

7

SELLING A CONDOMINIUM

Condominium selling is a little different from disposing of freehold property, and you should take careful note of the differences before putting yours on the market.

When you purchased this home, you were not buying real estate as such, but rather shares in a corporation, and your domain is the inner four walls. Beyond that, the areas are known as "common areas" and each tenant pays a monthly fee into a fund that takes care of real estate taxes and common area maintenance, which includes painting exteriors, grass cutting, snow removal, and general upkeep. By the way, your main selling point here is the fact that when you come home from work you can really put your feet up — no grass to cut, no peeling paintwork to worry about and in the winter, well, let it snow!

Getting back to the monthly fee, this money is administered by the board of directors, who are residents of the complex. In some instances, there is a "slush fund" contributed to by the residents for future development, such as some more tree planting or maybe a future swimming pool. While on the subject of this particular fund, it is well to note that when selling a condominium, the money that you have contributed to this pool remains after you leave. Once upon a time, the seller was able to take his or her portion.

The agreement for selling a condominium is basically similar to the one we have studied, but there are some additional items that should be noted. The chances are that you will not find a form dealing specifically with condominium selling, so you are going to have to "make do and mend" with the one you have.

The preamble which starts with the name of the purchasers, is usable for your purpose until you reach the section in which you would normally insert the municipal number. Instead of a street number, you would introduce the following:

> AND KNOWN AS Unit number 00 Condominium Plan Number 000 together with the Vendor's share of the undivided tenancy-in-common interest in the common elements as described in the declaration including the right to use such other parts of the common elements (there could be a swimming pool, recreation hall or children's playground, etc.).

Following this would come the purchase price and details of the down payment, all as in our previous example. The body of the document would include details of the mortgage financing, any special clauses or conditions just as for the freehold sale but with three additional comments that did not appear before.

"The common element maintenance fee is $000 per month, this payment including _____" and follow this with the items that this payment actually covers, for example, real estate taxes, electricity or whatever else is included. As always, be specific.

The second addition is, "This offer is conditional upon the purchasers being accepted as tenants by the board of directors."

Third, "this agreement is being made pursuant to the *condominium act for your province.*

I could go into a long and boring discourse on the various condominium acts, but it would serve no useful service and would not help you conclude a sale. The foregoing is all you need to know in order to complete your contract.

8

WHY DIDN'T THEY BUY?

Let us consider some of the reasons why your client did not buy, and I refer here to those people who were ready, willing and able, and not to those sightseers or those who just did not have the wherewithal to purchase your home.

Your advertising attracted them and convinced them to phone and eventually visit the property. So what went wrong? First, let us go back to the subject of advertising. You must agree that your advert attracted people, but did you overdo it? Did you glamorize your property too much? Is that "swimming pool in the back yard" a small, round, above-ground job instead of the kidney-shaped in-ground one that your advert led people to believe? Did the "well-treed lot" prove to consist of a couple of apple trees in the garden? Was that "oversized lot" just 30 metres deep? Of course, I am exaggerating here because I am trying to emphasize the importance of not being too wordy in your ads; keep them plain and simple, the way I have them in the example on page 22.

Over-emphasis leads people to believe that they are going to see a lot more than they eventually find. They end up horribly disappointed, and will no doubt leave you saying something like this: "Very nice. Thank you very much, we will be in touch." Go back to the chapter on advertising, follow the example, and then your visitors will be agreeably surprised. I reiterate here, forget that above-ground pool in the garden, let it be the unexpected goodie. I can well remember having a house for sale with a beautiful pool in the back garden, and in my first advert I made no mention of this whatever. My vendor phoned quite upset because I had omitted this fact. I replied that this was a deliberate omission, and I requested that when I brought a couple of prospects through that evening the drapes at the rear of the house be closed. I showed my people through the home and by the time I had reached the living room, which was the best feature, they were duly impressed. When I threw open the drapes, however, revealing a sparkling pool, that clinched it. This was something they had not expected, and was the feature that sold the house. So you see from this that it is far better to underplay what you have to offer than to over-emphasize.

In your advertisement, however, you had copied the example. You itemized private sale, location, price, type of house, and number of bedrooms, as recommended. Then, go back to the discourse on answering the phone. Remember that this is all part and parcel of the advertising campaign. Were you too wordy? Did you over-enthuse? You can indicate over the phone that the property has much more to offer than it actually has. Refer back to the chapter on answering the phone (see page 25), and in this you will note that I suggested you make no comments other than replying to the questions asked.

However, you followed the instructions explicitly and your prospects arrived, not expecting a palace, but just the type of home they were looking for. It was in their price range and they liked the location, but *still* did not buy. Perhaps you were confused over your facts and figures. Nothing will put people off more than uncertainty; they begin to doubt your credibility, and if you prove to be wrong in some little thing they wonder how far off course you are in the bigger, more important matters. Bear in mind that these people are probably making the biggest investment they will ever make in their lives, and they want to be very sure of their facts. Do not be ashamed to have that clip board on your knee. No one will object to your being a human being, rather than a computer; in fact, it is a good idea to turn the board towards them, with a "Yes, here you see the taxes were $856 last year," or "Our electricity bill, as you can see, was $30 per month." In many cases, seeing it down in black and white is more convincing; at least they can see that you have been doing your homework.

But the question period went swimmingly; in fact, they were very impressed by the knowledge you displayed during the tour of the house. You didn't miss a trick. If this be the case, now let us consider the actual showing. Was it orderly? Was it conducted by one person? Were the family and animals trailing along? Was there loud music? Any smells? Yes, smells, let us not forget these. We become accustomed to our own odors and do not notice them, so if there was garlic for supper, or boiled cabbage, or some greasy fried concoction, get busy with that air cleaner. You may well ask, "If a prospect really liked the house, would an odor put him off?" You can bet your life it would. I found a house for a young couple that was everything they wanted, including the right price. On the evening that I showed them through, mother was in the kitchen frying up a mess of veal cutlets in oil and garlic. My people could not get out of the house fast enough; in fact, I thought that they were going to be sick. No amount of explanation on my part would have convinced them that this was the home for them.

Remember, I already noted in this book that trying to make a sale is like walking a tight rope; the least little thing can tip the balance. While on the subject of smells, here are a couple of little tricks you could adopt. Most commercial air cleaners are somewhat overpowering, so try some natural pleasant odors, perhaps a cinnamon bun in the oven or a coffee pot bubbling away in the kitchen.

The showing went over very well, the house smelled like a spring garden, everything sparkled, the prospects were just about as enthused as they could possibly be, but still walked out of the house without buying, although they did say that they would be back. It must be that your sale closing attempt was inadequate. In the next chapter, I will discuss closing the sale.

9

CLOSING THE SALE

a. WHEN THEY'RE ALMOST ON THE HOOK

First of all, we must discuss those buyer signals again; people giving them out are the ones to zero in on. Do not waste any time on the obviously uninterested; the best salesperson in the world will not sell a woman on a kitchen she hates, so do not bother to try.

We have at last reached the stage when we know that our prospect is "ready, willing and able," as they have been signalling all over the place. "Jane would simply love this room . . . I would change the color of this . . . my living room suite would go beautifully with this carpet . . . I would get rid of that tree in the front . . . your desk would fit just right in that corner," and the best one of all, "We would like to move in before the children go back to school."

I am assuming that, following my advice, you are back in the best room in the house, and after socializing a little are ready to talk business. At this stage, your prospective purchasers have no knowledge of the fact that you have the ability to draw up the offer and complete the necessary paperwork. They are still under the impression that they have to consult their lawyer; in fact one of them will most likely say, "We will see our lawyer on Monday morning."

This is the point at which you could lose them. Everything has gone swimmingly thus far, but remember that if you let them out of that front door without obtaining a commitment from them, that tightrope is going to start swaying. Once they have gone, even if they have every intention of going through with the deal, all kinds of things can happen. They may see another house that they like better, they may have a change of heart because the school is a little farther away than they thought, or after sleeping on it they get cold feet. Your reply to the seeing-the-lawyer-or-Uncle-Fred-or-whoever-bit, should be as follows: "We do have a number of very interested people and I would like to get this settled over the weekend. Are you interested enough to give us an offer?" The reply could be, "You are asking $61 500 . . . would you be interested in say, $60 000?" As this is the price you had in mind, you agree that $60 000 would be fine.

At this point, they may offer to give you a cheque as a deposit, rather as if they were buying a car or a refrigerator, or some thing of this nature, and in pulling out the cheque book may say, "I will give you five hundred now and see my lawyer on Monday." This, of course, is of little value in a real estate transaction without the required documentation. You must also bear in mind that if a change of heart does occur, a cheque can be easily stopped, so you have no safeguard whatsoever. At this point, you must gently persuade your prospect to complete an agreement with you. Produce the document and go through it, explaining what it is all about. If, after this discourse, they still demur and insist upon seeing a lawyer before signing anything, you can then point out that this fact can be written right into the offer and is done so in the following fashion:

"This offer is conditional upon the approval of the purchasers' lawyer, Charles Crook. Failure to obtain such approval renders this offer null and void and the purchasers' deposit returned to them in full without interest or deduction."

It is important that the lawyer's name be spelled out as this narrows down the chances of your clients wriggling off the hook. All they would have to do, if they changed their mind, is to phone you and say that their lawyer disapproved. By the way, do not forget to have the deposit cheque made out to your lawyer's trust account.

It may appear that I am being somewhat over-cautious in the above, but through bitter experience I have learned that there is no such thing as over-caution in matters contractual.

If, despite all this, your prospective purchasers still refuse to commit themselves to paper, make up the offer anyway (there is nothing much else you can do), hand it to them, unsigned by you, of course, at the same time letting them know that the property is still on the market, and that if you do receive an acceptable offer in writing you will have to sign it. The chances are that this last remark may create some deep thinking on their part and you could very well receive a telephone call that evening to say that they are willing to sign. This is the value in giving them the completed document; they have had an opportunity to peruse it and realise that without the lawyer's or Uncle Fred's approval, they are indeed off the hook.

Well, anyway, you have done the best you can, and all you can do from now on is to keep your fingers crossed and continue showing the house.

b. THE BEST OF LUCK!

In this vast land of ours there are many levels of government, so we have many variables. It would be quite impossible, within the covers of one book, to list these differences, so what I have tried to do is to give you all the basics. Following the steps that I have set out will, I know, help you sell your own home. I am quite certain for instance that the agreement I have set out would be a viable contract anywhere. If there are any changes or differences, however, your lawyer would very quickly point them out. "Hey, we don't do that like this!" "What nitwit told you to write it down this way?"

Do not worry or be put off by this; you have your purchaser's signature on a document and this is the most important thing. So whether you are selling an igloo up north, or a cottage on an island, the basic rules of the game are the same. You will still have to make it shine, still need to know your facts and figures, still have to price it right, and still know how to advertise. The smell of blubber in the igloo or rotting oysters on the island, which should have been taken care of before showing the property, can still be a deterrent in the selling process, in the same way that greasy garlic can be anywhere in between. Remember that, wherever you are, people have similar likes and dislikes.

GLOSSARY

In order to help make you as knowledgeable as possible, I have compiled a list of some of the terms that you may hear during your real estate efforts, and it is as well to know what they mean. As I have often stated, the more you know, the more confidence you will inspire in your prospect. This is a most important factor in the bringing of your transaction to a successful conclusion.

ABSTRACT
The written history of your property as held at the registry office. (For a very modest sum you can peruse this document, and it might be as well to do so prior to putting your place on the market)

AGREEMENT OF PURCHASE AND SALE
A contract for the purchase and sale of real estate

AMORTIZATION
The repayment of a mortgage loan by equal and regular monthly payments

APPRAISAL
An opinion or estimate of market value

APPURTENANCES
The rights that go with a property

ASSESSED VALUE
Valuation placed on real estate by the local municipality for taxation purposes

CAVEAT EMPTOR
A Latin phrase which means "Let the buyer beware"

CHATTELS
Things that can be removed from a property without causing any damage

CLOUD ON TITLE
Any claim against a property (A mortgage could be considered a "cloud.")

CONDOMINIUM
Separate ownership of units in a multiple unit situation, with separate deeds and mortgages

CONSIDERATION
Valuable consideration — in real estate transactions this is usually money

CONTRACT
An agreement between two or more people to do, or not to do, something

DEED
A legal document or instrument that is used to convey property to a purchaser

DEPOSIT
Valuable consideration as a pledge for the fulfilment of a contract, and in real estate transactions becomes part of the purchase price

DEPRECIATION
The decrease in value of a property in the course of time

DOWER
The rights of a wife in the husband's property

EASEMENT
A right of way that permits passage through and use of land by a non-owner. (Easements are usually granted to telephone companies or public utility people to enable them to service their equipment)

ENCUMBRANCE
An outstanding claim against a property or the legal right of a non-owner to use of a property

EQUITY
The difference between the market value of a property and what is owing on it in the form of mortgages, etc.

EQUITY OF REDEMPTION
The right of the mortgage borrower to pay the mortgage in full and so obtain full ownership of it

EXTRAS
Chattels or moveable goods that are to remain with the property when it is sold

FEE SIMPLE
The ultimate ownership of property (The term means that it is free of all liens and encumbrances.)

FIXTURES
Those items that are attached to a building that may not be removed by the vendor

INSTRUMENT
A legal document such as a deed

JOINT TENANCY
Ownership of property by two people, where on the death of one party the whole reverts to the survivor

LIEN
Any cloud or encumbrance on the title

MARKET VALUE
The price a knowledgeable purchaser would pay to an equally knowledgeable vendor for the piece of property

MECHANICS LIEN
A claim against a property for labor or materials that have

not been paid for (You can sometimes have this kind of a lien against your property and have no knowledge of the fact. This points up the importance of checking through your abstract before putting the house up for sale.)

MORTGAGE
A sum of money loaned with real estate as a security for payment

MORTGAGEE
The person or organization that lends the money (the lender)

MORTGAGOR
The person who borrows the money and is responsible for making the payments (the borrower)

OPTION
The right given by a vendor to a purchaser to buy a property within a given time (There is a deposit required in this form of transaction. In option to purchase contracts, it is usually a case of someone renting a property with an option to buy within, say, one year. The purchaser has to pay a certain deposit or valuable consideration. If, however, the purchaser does not pick up this option within that given time, he or she loses the deposit.)

PERSONAL PROPERTY
Everything except land and the buildings thereon and, of course, the fixtures

REAL ESTATE
The actual lands and the buildings thereon

REAL PROPERTY
Real estate (It may also include the benefits that go with it, such as peaceful tenancy and the intangible values.)

SURVEY
The accurate measurements of the lot that are recorded on
the deed

TENANTS IN COMMON
Ownership of property by two or more people where if one
party dies, his or her share of the lands goes to his or her
estate

TITLE
Proof of ownership

NOTES

NOTES

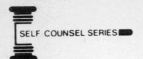

ORDER FORM
SELF-COUNSEL SERIES

SELF COUNSEL SERIES

5/80

NATIONAL TITLES:

Adopted?	3.95
Becoming a Canadian	3.50
Changing Your Name in Canada	3.50
Civil Rights in Canada	2.50
Consumer Law in Canada	2.50
Collecting Debts Successfully	3.50
Credit Law and Bankruptcy Handbook	3.95
Drinking and Driving	4.50
Energy, Money & Your Future	4.95
Exporting	9.95
Federal Incorporation and Business Guide	11.95
Future of Money	2.95
Immigrating to Canada	7.95
Immigrating to the U.S.A.	7.95
Importing	19.95
Insuring Business Risks	3.50
Life Insurance for Canadians	2.95
Mike Grenby's Tax Tips	3.50
Mike Grenby's Money Book	4.50
Our Accountant's Guide for the Small Business	4.50
Public Speaking	4.95
Runaway Inflation	2.95
Retirement Guide for Canadians	5.95
Starting a Successful Business in Canada	6.95
Successful Job-Hunting in Canada	1.95
Tax Shelters in Canada	4.95
Trusts and Trust Companies	3.95
War on Gold	4.95
What to Do When the Taxman Comes	3.95

PROVINCIAL TITLES:

Divorce Guide
☐B.C. 6.95 ☐Alberta 6.95 ☐Ontario 8.50 ☐Man./Sask. 7.95

Employee/Employer Rights
☐B.C. 3.95 ☐Alberta 2.95 ☐Ontario 2.95

Marriage & Family Law
☐B.C. 5.95 ☐Alberta 5.95 ☐Ontario 4.95

Fight That Ticket
☐B.C. 3.50 ☐Alberta 2.95 ☐Ontario 2.50

Incorporation Guide
☐B.C. 9.95 ☐Alberta 9.95 ☐Ontario 9.95 ☐Man./Sask. 9.95

Landlord/Tenant Rights
☐B.C. 4.95 ☐Alberta 3.50 ☐Ontario 4.95

Real Estate Guide
☐B.C. 4.95   ☐Alberta 3.95   ☐Ontario 4.95

Small Claims Court Guide
☐B.C. 4.50   ☐Alberta 2.50   ☐Ontario 3.95

Probate Guide
☐B.C. 11.95   ☐Alberta 9.95   ☐Ontario 9.95

Wills
☐B.C. 3.95   ☐Alberta 3.50   ☐Ontario 3.95

Wills/Probate Procedure
☐Sask./Man. 3.50

PACKAGED FORMS:

Incorporation
☐B.C. 9.95   ☐Alberta 7.95   ☐Ontario 8.50   ☐Man./Sask. 7.95

Divorce
☐B.C. 6.95   ☐Alberta 7.95   ☐Ontario 11.95☐Man. 8.50   ☐Sask. 12.50

Probate
☐B.C. 11.95   ☐Alberta 11.95   ☐Ontario 11.50

Sell Your Own Home
☐B.C. 3.95   ☐Alberta 3.95   ☐Ontario 3.95

Rental Form Kit (B.C., Alberta, Ontario, Man.Sask.)   3.50

Have Your Made Your Will?   **4.95**

If You Love Me Put It In Writing   9.95

Expense Form Kit   7.95

NOTE: All prices subject to change without notice.

Cheque or Money Order
(plus sales tax where applicable) enclosed.

(PLEASE PRINT)

Name _____

Address _____

City _____

Province _____

Postal Code _____

If order is under $6.00, add 50¢ for postage and handling.

Please send orders to:

INTERNATIONAL SELF-COUNSEL PRESS LTD.
306 West 25th Street
North Vancouver, British Columbia
V7N 2G1